BONSAI FOR BEGINNERS

From Novice to Expert-The Comprehensive Guide to Cultivating, Pruning and Nurturing Your First Bonsai with Detailed Expert Techniques and Insights.|BONUS: Pruning Tutorial

MOSAIC MILLS PUBLISHING-

© Copyright 2024 by MOSAIC MILLS PUBLISHING - All rights reserved.

The following Book is reproduced below with the goal of providing information that is as accurate and reliable as possible. Regardless, purchasing this Book can be seen as consent to the fact that both the publisher and the author of this Book are in no way experts on the topics discussed within and that any recommendations or suggestions that are made herein are for entertainment purposes only. Professionals should be consulted as needed prior to undertaking any of the action endorsed herein.

This declaration is deemed fair and valid by both the American Bar Association and the Committee of Publishers Association and is legally binding throughout the United States.

Furthermore, the transmission, duplication, or reproduction of any of the following work including specific information will be considered an illegal act irrespective of if it is done electronically or in print. This extends to creating a secondary or tertiary copy of the work or a recorded copy and is only allowed with the express written consent from the Publisher. All additional right reserved.

The information in the following pages is broadly considered a truthful and accurate account of facts and as such, any inattention, use, or misuse of the information in question by the reader will render any resulting actions solely under their purview. There are no scenarios in which the publisher or the original author of this work can be in any fashion deemed liable for any hardship or damages that may befall them after undertaking information described herein.

Additionally, the information in the following pages is intended only for informational purposes and should thus be thought of as universal. As befitting its nature, it is presented without assurance regarding its prolonged validity or interim quality. Trademarks that are mentioned are done without written consent and can in no way be considered an endorsement from the trademark holder.

Contents

- INTRODUCTION 12
- **CHAPTER 1: BONSAI: A MINIATURE WORLD** 13
  - Introduction To Chapter 1 13
  - 1.1 History And Origins Of Bonsai 13
    - Origins in ancient china 13
    - Transition to japan and the birth of bonsai 13
    - Bonsai's cultural evolution in japan 14
    - Bonsai in the western world 14
    - Modern bonsai and global influence 14
  - 1.2 Philosophy And Cultural Significance 15
    - Philosophical foundations 15
    - Cultural significance 15
    - Bonsai in the modern context 15
  - 1.3 Bonsai In The Modern World 16
    - Adaptation and evolution 16
    - Globalization and community building 17
    - Technological advancements 17
    - Challenges and opportunities 17
- **CHAPTER 2: THE FIRST STEP: CHOOSING YOUR PLANT** 19
  - 2.1 Ideal Species For Beginners 19
  - Disclaimer: Enhancing The Beauty Of Bonsai Through Imagery 20
    - Ficus (ficus spp.) 21
    - Juniper (juniperus spp.) 22
    - Chinese elm (ulmus parvifolia) 23
    - Dwarf schefflera (schefflera arboricola) 24
  - 2.2 Understanding Climate And Environment 25
    - Climate zones and bonsai selection 25
    - Temperature and seasonal changes 25
    - Sunlight and shade requirements 25
    - Humidity and air circulation 25
    - Soil and water considerations 25
    - Adapting to indoor environments 26

  Local pests and diseases 26

2.3 Bonsai Selection Criteria 26

2.4 Other Common Bonsai Species 28

  Japanese Maple (Acer palmatum) 28

  Fukien Tea (Carmona) 29

  Jade Plant (Crassula or portulacaria) 30

  Azalea (Rhododendron) 31

  Bougainvillea 32

  Serissa (Serissa Foetida) 33

  Boxwood (Buxus) 34

  Chinese Sweet Plum (Sageretia Theezans) 35

  Olive Tree (Olea Europaea) 36

  Money Tree (Pachira Aquatica) 37

  Privet (Ligustrum) 38

  Cotoneaster 39

  Lemon and Orange Trees (Citrus Limon and Sinensis) 40

  Brazilian Rain Tree (Pithecellobium tortum) 41

  Brush Cerry (Eugenia myrtifolia and syzygium) 42

  Fuchsia 43

  Japanese Holly (Ilex Crenata) 44

  Premna 45

  Gardenia 46

  Crape Myrtle (Lagerstroemia Indica) 47

  Common Myrtle (Myrtus Communis) 48

  Pyracantha 49

  Water Jasmine (Wrightia Religiosa) 50

  Acacia 51

  Camellia 52

  Bamboo (Bambusoideae) 53

  Hibiscus 54

  Eucalyptus 55

  Lilac (Syringa) 56

    Ming aralia (Polyscias Fruticosa) 57

    Rosemary (Rosemarinus) 58

CHAPTER 3: WATER: THE ELIXIR OF LIFE FOR BONSAI 59

3.1 Irrigation Techniques 59

    Understanding your bonsai's water needs 59

    Watering techniques 59

    Frequency and timing of watering 60

    Water quality 60

    Avoiding common watering mistakes 60

3.2 Managing Humidity And Dryness 60

    Understanding the role of humidity 60

    Dealing with dry air 61

    Monitoring and adjusting 61

3.3 Common Signs Of Watering Issues 61

    Identifying overwatering 61

    Recognizing under-watering 62

    Responsive watering practices 62

CHAPTER 4: LIGHT AND SHADOW: POSITIONING YOUR BONSAI 63

4.1 Light Requirements For Different Species 63

    General light requirements in bonsai 63

    Light requirements for specific bonsai species 63

    Practical examples 64

4.2 Best Practices For Placement 64

4.3 Effects Of Light On Growth 65

CHAPTER 5: DETERMINE YOUR CLIMATE, AMOUNT OF SPACE, DEGREE OF LIGHT, AND BREEZE—AND WHICH TREES MAY WORK BETTER IN DIFFERENT CLIMATES? 67

    Assessing your environment: 67

    Finding your climate zone: 67

    Selecting Trees for Different Climates: 68

    Considerations 68

CHAPTER 6: THE FERTILIZING PROCESS FOR BONSAI 69

6.1 Understanding Bonsai Fertilizer 69

6.2 Assessing Your Bonsai's Nutritional Needs 69

6.3 Fertilizing Techniques 70

6.4 Over-Fertilizing And Under-Fertilizing: 70

6.5 Special Considerations For Different Bonsai Styles 70

6.6 Fertilizing Newly Repotted Or Sick Bonsai 71

Conclusion 71

CHAPTER 7: OVERWINTERING BONSAI: ENSURING YOUR TREES THRIVE THROUGH WINTER 72

7.1 Understanding Bonsai Dormancy 72

7.2 Preparing For Winter 72

Winter Care for Outdoor Bonsai: 72

Winter Care for Indoor Bonsai: 73

7.3 Monitoring And Maintenance Through Winter 73

7.4 Spring Recovery 74

7.5 Special Considerations 74

Conclusion 75

CHAPTER 8: PATIENCE AND CARE: GROWING YOUR BONSAI 76

8.1 Long-Term Development Of The Bonsai 76

The evolution of form and character 76

Adapting care over time 77

The role of patience and observation 77

The rewards of long-term cultivation 77

8.2 Managing The Bonsai Across Seasons 77

Spring: a time of awakening 77

Summer: vigilance and growth 78

Autumn: preparing for rest 78

Winter: dormancy and protection 78

CHAPTER 9: HEALING AND PROTECTING: MANAGING PESTS AND DISEASES 79

9.1 Identifying Common Pests 79

Aphids 79

Spider mites 79

Scale insects 80

Mealybugs 80

Whiteflies 80

- Fungus gnats 80
- Preventive measures and initial responses 80
- Treatment strategies for common pests 81
- Regular monitoring and maintenance 81
- Preventive measures 81

9.2 Prevention And Treatment Of Diseases 82
Common Bonsai Diseases 82
Prevention Strategies 82
Treatment Of Diseases 82
Recovery And Aftercare 83

9.3 Long-Term Health Of The Bonsai 83
- Regular health checks 83
- Soil and root care 84
- Nutrition and fertilization 84
- Environmental factors 84
- Pruning and training 84
- Stress management 84
- Long-term planning 84

CHAPTER 10: THE MAGIC OF PRUNING: SCULPTING YOUR BONSAI 86

10.1 Fundamentals Of Pruning 86
- Understanding growth patterns 86
- Tools for pruning 86
- Techniques of pruning 87
- Timing of pruning 87
- Pruning for shape and style 87
- Healing and aftercare 87
- Developing a pruning strategy 87

10.2 Training And Shaping Techniques 88
- Wiring 88
- Wiring Tips and Techniques 89
- Pruning 90
- Clipping and pinching 90

- Grafting 91
- Defoliation 91
- Creating deadwood 91

10.3 Maintenance And Aesthetic Care 92

CHAPTER 11: STYLES AND FORMS: ARTISTIC EXPRESSION IN BONSAI 94

11.1 Overview Of Bonsai Styles 94

- Formal upright (chokkan) 95
- Informal upright (moyogi) 97
- Broom (hokidachi) 99
- Slanting (shakan) 101
- Windswept (fukinagashi) 103
- Twin trunk (sokan) 105
- Clump (kabudachi) 107
- Forest (Yose-ue) 109
- Raft (Ikada-buki) 111
- Cascade (kengai) 113
- Semi-cascade (han-kengai) 115
- In rock (ishitsuki) 117
- Literati (bunjin) 119
- Driftwood (sharimiki) 121

11.2 Creating Specific Styles 123

- Understanding the Tree's Natural Inclinations 123
- The Role of Pruning in Shaping 123
- Wiring and Training 123
- Incorporating Aesthetics and Balance 123
- Adapting and Experimenting 123
- Patience and Persistence 124
- Reflecting on the Artistic Journey 124
- Embracing the Evolution 124
- The Joy of Sharing 124

11.3 Creativity And Personal Expression In Bonsai 124

CHAPTER 12: REPOTTING: RENEWING YOUR BONSAI'S ROOTS 126

12.1 When And How To Repot 126

12.2 Selecting Soil And Pots 127

    The art of choosing soil 127

    Selecting the right pot 128

    The harmony of soil and pot 128

CHAPTER 13: THE BONSAIST'S WORKSHOP: ESSENTIAL TOOLS AND MATERIALS 129

13.1 Overview Of Necessary Tools 129

    Pruning tools 129

    Wiring tools 130

    Soil and repotting tools 130

    Miscellaneous tools 130

13.2 Maintenance And Care Of Tools 130

    Cleaning and sharpening 130

    Storage and handling 131

    Replacement and professional servicing 131

13.3 Supplementary Materials For Bonsai 131

    Soil mixes 131

    Wires for shaping 131

    Fertilizers 132

    Moss and decorative elements 132

    Drainage and humidity trays 132

CHAPTER 14: FROM SEED TO SPLENDOR: CULTIVATING YOUR BONSAI 133

14.1 Propagation From Seed 133

    Understanding seed selection 133

    The stratification process 133

    Sowing techniques 133

    Initial Care and Germination 133

    Patience and Observation 134

14.2 Initial Growth And Cultivation 134

    Transition from Seedling to Sapling 134

    Soil and Watering Considerations 134

    First Steps in Training and Pruning 134

- Adapting to the Plant's Needs 134
- Building a Strong Foundation 135

CHAPTER 15: EXPERT ADVICE: AVOIDING COMMON MISTAKES 136

15.1 Frequent Beginner Errors 136
- Overwatering and underwatering 136
- Neglecting light requirements 136
- Improper pruning 136
- Choosing the wrong soil mix 137
- Misunderstanding fertilization 137
- Ignoring pest and disease signs 137

15.3 Advanced Tips And Techniques 137
- Mastering advanced pruning techniques 137
- Refining wiring skills 138
- Root pruning and repotting 138
- Soil composition and fertilization 138
- Climate and environmental adaptation 138
- Artistic and creative development 139
- Continuous learning and experimentation 139
- Balancing aesthetics and health 139
- Advanced soil management 139
- Advanced display techniques 140
- Lifelong learning and adaptation 140

CHAPTER 16: SOURCING BONSAI MATERIAL 142
16.1 In My First Year, What Should I Focus On Or Prioritize My Investment? 143

CHAPTER 17: EXPLORE THE WORLD OF BONSAI ON YOUTUBE 145

CONCLUSION 146

Thank you for purchasing this book.

Scan the QR code to download your bonuses and leave a review.

We, independent publishing houses, need your opinion, and by making this small gesture, you will give us a chance to be more visible than the big publishers. *Thank you so much for taking the time to do this.*

TO DOWNLOAD THE PRUNING TUTORIAL GUIDE:

TO DOWNLOAD THE FULL-COLOR VERSION:

TO LEAVE US A REVIEW:

INTRODUCTION

Welcome to "BONSAI FOR BEGINNERS," a comprehensive guide designed to introduce you to the captivating world of Bonsai. This book is your companion on a journey into the art and science of cultivating these miniature trees, an ancient practice that combines horticultural skills with artistic creativity.

Bonsai, a tradition with deep roots in Asian culture, is more than just a gardening practice; it's a form of living art that captures the beauty and spirit of nature in a small, harmonious form. This book is crafted to guide beginners and enthuses seasoned practitioners alike, offering a blend of practical advice, step-by-step techniques, and philosophical insights.

Structured into ten detailed chapters, each section of this book delves into a specific aspect of bonsai cultivation. From the history and philosophy of Bonsai to the practicalities of selection, pruning, watering, and repotting, we cover every element essential to beginning and nurturing your bonsai journey. You'll learn about managing light and shadow, tackling pests and diseases, and understanding the nuances of different bonsai styles and forms.

Our approach is to make the art of Bonsai accessible and enjoyable for everyone. The language used throughout the book is clear and free from excessive jargon, ensuring that concepts are easy to grasp. We believe learning about Bonsai should be as serene and enjoyable as the practice.

Each chapter is meticulously structured to provide in-depth information and practical tips.

"BONSAI FOR BEGINNERS" is more than just a guide; it's a source of inspiration. It encourages you to see Bonsai not just as a hobby, but as a path to deeper appreciation of nature's beauty and an exercise in patience and creativity. Whether you're taking your first steps into Bonsai or looking to deepen your existing knowledge, this book is designed to guide, inspire, and empower you on your bonsai journey.

Let's embark on this journey together, exploring the delicate balance of nature and artistry, and discover the joy and fulfillment that comes from growing Bonsai.

CHAPTER 1: BONSAI: A MINIATURE WORLD

Introduction To Chapter 1

Embark on a journey into the captivating world of Bonsai, an art form that encapsulates the beauty and complexity of nature in miniature. This first chapter of "BONSAI FOR BEGINNERS" is designed to introduce you to the rich history, cultural significance, and modern practice of Bonsai. Here, we unravel the origins of Bonsai, explore its philosophical underpinnings, and examine how this ancient art form has evolved and flourished in contemporary settings. Whether you are a curious beginner or a bonsai enthusiast, this chapter will deepen your appreciation of Bonsai and provide a solid foundation for your bonsai journey.

1.1 History And Origins Of Bonsai

The art of Bonsai, a captivating blend of nature and craftsmanship, has a rich and nuanced history that spans over a thousand years and crosses many cultural boundaries. This journey into the past helps us appreciate the art form and informs our contemporary practice of Bonsai.

Origins in ancient china

The earliest known practice that resembles Bonsai originated in China during the Tang Dynasty (618-907 AD). This art, known as "penjing," involved the creation of miniature landscapes. These landscapes were more than just small trees; they were entire scenes crafted to represent natural landscapes in diminutive form. Rocks, water features, and figurines were often incorporated to create these scenes, known as "tray landscapes."

Penjing was deeply influenced by Chinese philosophies, particularly Taoism, which emphasized harmony between humans and nature. This art form was seen as a way to capture the natural world's profound and often elusive beauty, making it accessible within the confines of a small space. The practice of penjing was not just horticultural but also a spiritual and artistic endeavor, reflecting the Taoist pursuit of harmony and balance.

Transition to japan and the birth of bonsai

The practice of cultivating miniature trees was introduced to Japan from China through trade and cultural exchanges during the Kamakura period (1185–1333). The Japanese refined and reinterpreted these techniques, giving birth to what we now know as Bonsai. The term "bonsai" itself translates to "planted in a container."

In Japan, Bonsai became intertwined with Zen Buddhism, which was influential during this period. The Zen Buddhist principles of simplicity, mindfulness, and the appreciation of natural beauty significantly shaped the Japanese approach to Bonsai. Unlike the Chinese penjing, which focused on landscapes, Japanese Bonsai primarily focused on individual trees. This shift was significant, as it emphasized the idea of representing the whole of nature in a single tree, a concept deeply rooted in Zen philosophy.

The Japanese approach to Bonsai also reflected the aesthetic principles of wabi-sabi, which finds beauty in imperfection, transience, and simplicity. Bonsai, in this context, became a symbol of harmony, peace, and balance. It was no longer just a representation of nature but also an expression of philosophical and artistic ideals.

Bonsai's cultural evolution in japan

Over centuries, Bonsai in Japan evolved from being a practice of Buddhist monks and the elite to becoming a popular hobby for people of various social strata. During the Edo period (1603-1868), Bonsai began to see changes in styles and techniques, becoming more sophisticated and varied. This period also saw the development of specialized tools, pots, and cultivation methods, which further refined the art.

The Tokugawa shogunate's policy of isolation (sakoku) during this era inadvertently nurtured Bonsai's growth within Japan, leading to unique styles and techniques distinct from its Chinese roots. Bonsai became a symbol of prestige and was often used in diplomatic contexts, reflecting a deep cultural appreciation for the art.

Bonsai in the western world

The international debut of Bonsai occurred during the Paris World Exhibition in 1900. This was a pivotal moment, as it introduced the Western world to the art of Bonsai, sparking interest and fascination. Subsequent international exhibitions in London (1910) and New York (1915) further exposed Bonsai to a global audience.

The 20th century saw a significant expansion of Bonsai from Japan to the rest of the world. Post-World War II, as international travel and communication increased, so did the global interest in and practice of Bonsai. Western practitioners began to take up Bonsai, adapting the art to local conditions and tree species, which led to a diversification of styles and techniques.

Modern bonsai and global influence

Today, Bonsai is a global art form practiced by enthusiasts in almost every country. Modern Bonsai has been influenced by its international practitioners, leading to innovative styles and techniques that respect the art's traditional roots while also reflecting the diverse environments and cultures where it thrives.

Bonsai societies, clubs, and exhibitions have sprung up worldwide, fostering a community of practitioners who share knowledge, techniques, and their love for this art form. The internet has played a crucial role in this, allowing for an unprecedented exchange of ideas and furthering the evolution of Bonsai.

In summary, the history of Bonsai is a testament to the art's enduring appeal and its ability to adapt and evolve across different cultures and eras. From its origins in ancient China to its refinement in Japan and its eventual spread across the globe, Bonsai has continually captivated people with its unique blend of natural beauty and artistic expression. This journey through time highlights not only the horticultural skills involved in Bonsai but also the deeper philosophical and cultural significance that makes it a truly global art form.

As we move forward in this book, we will delve into the practical aspects of bonsai cultivation. However, it's important to remember that every technique and principle is steeped in this rich history. Understanding the origins and evolution of Bonsai enriches our practice and connects us to the countless generations of artists and gardeners who have shaped this living art form.

1.2 Philosophy And Cultural Significance

As we delve deeper into the world of Bonsai, it becomes evident that this art form is much more than the cultivation of miniature trees. It is deeply rooted in philosophical concepts and cultural significance that transcend its aesthetic appeal.

Philosophical foundations

The philosophy of Bonsai is intrinsically linked to Asia's broader philosophical and spiritual traditions, particularly those of Zen Buddhism and Taoism. These philosophies emphasize harmony with nature, mindfulness, and the pursuit of spiritual balance.

Zen Buddhism and Mindfulness: In Zen Buddhism, every action can be a path to mindfulness and enlightenment. Bonsai, with its meticulous and deliberate care, becomes a meditative practice. The slow, thoughtful shaping of a bonsai tree is an exercise in patience and attentiveness. Each cut and adjustment is a mindful act, reflecting the Zen principle of being fully present in the moment.

Taoism and Harmony with Nature: Taoism's influence is evident in the way bonsai artists strive to create a natural and harmonious appearance. The Taoist concept of 'wu wei' (effortless action) is mirrored in Bonsai, where the goal is to work with the tree's natural tendencies, not against them. This approach fosters a deep connection with the natural world, encouraging an understanding of the rhythms and patterns of nature.

Cultural significance

Bonsai has held a significant place in various cultures, particularly in China and Japan, where it originated and evolved.

Symbolism and Aesthetics in Chinese Culture: Penjing (the precursor to Bonsai) was laden with symbolic meanings in Chinese culture. Different elements in a penjing composition represented various aspects of life and nature. For instance, rocks could symbolize mountains, or a gnarled tree could represent longevity and resilience. The aesthetic appeal was tied to these symbolic representations, making penjing a form of storytelling as much as gardening.

Japanese Aesthetics and Wabi-Sabi: Bonsai became part of the broader aesthetic and cultural tradition in Japan. It is closely associated with the concept of wabi-sabi, which finds beauty in simplicity, impermanence, and imperfection. A bonsai tree embodies this aesthetic with its asymmetrical shape, visible scars, and unforced beauty. It represents the natural world in its true form – imperfect, transient, yet profoundly beautiful.

Bonsai in the modern context

In contemporary times, Bonsai continues to hold significant cultural and philosophical importance, transcending its traditional East Asian roots to gain a global following. This widespread appeal can be attributed to several factors:

Global Symbol of Peace and Perseverance: Bonsai trees are often seen as symbols of peace, resilience, and the enduring power of nature. This symbolism has universal appeal, resonating with people across different cultures and backgrounds. The art of Bonsai, requiring years of dedicated care, symbolizes commitment, patience, and the ability to thrive under challenging conditions.

Artistic Expression and Personal Growth: Bonsai cultivation has evolved into a form of personal artistic expression. Each bonsai tree reflects its creator's unique style and vision, making each tree a personal artwork. This aspect of Bonsai aligns with the contemporary emphasis on individual creativity and self-expression.

Connection to Nature in Urban Settings: Bonsai offers a way to maintain a connection to nature as the world becomes more urbanized. In bustling cities where gardens are a luxury, a bonsai tree provides a living piece of nature. This connection is increasingly important as people seek ways to balance urban living with a need for natural beauty and tranquility.

Educational and Therapeutic Value: Bonsai cultivation is being recognized for its educational and therapeutic benefits. It teaches biological principles, horticultural skills, and environmental awareness. Therapeutically, the practice of Bonsai has been found to reduce stress, improve mental well-being, and enhance physical dexterity.

Cultural Exchange and Community Building: The global bonsai community is a vibrant example of cultural exchange and shared passion. Bonsai clubs, forums, and exhibitions bring together people from diverse backgrounds, fostering a sense of community and mutual learning. This aspect of bonsai culture is powerful in promoting understanding and appreciation across cultural boundaries.

Bonsai's philosophy and cultural significance are as deep and varied as art. From its roots in Asian philosophies to its modern interpretations and applications, Bonsai remains a profound expression of the human connection to nature and an art form that speaks to our shared human experience.

1.3 Bonsai In The Modern World

This journey will take us through the evolution of Bonsai in contemporary times, its integration into different cultures, and the role technology and globalization play in shaping the future of this timeless practice.

Adaptation and evolution

The transition of Bonsai from traditional East Asian art to a global phenomenon has been marked by significant adaptation and evolution.

Diversification of Styles and Techniques: Modern bonsai artists have introduced innovative styles and techniques while traditional bonsai styles are still revered and practiced. These variations are often influenced by the local climate, native tree species, and individual artistic expression, leading to a richer and more diverse bonsai tradition.

Incorporation of Non-Traditional Species: In addition to traditional species like pines, maples, and junipers, modern bonsai practitioners have begun experimenting with a variety of non-traditional species. This diversification allows Bonsai to be more accessible globally, as enthusiasts can work with species better suited to their local environments.

Globalization and community building

Advancements in communication and transportation have facilitated the spread of Bonsai across the globe.

International Bonsai Community: The internet has played a crucial role in connecting bonsai enthusiasts worldwide. Online forums, social media groups, and digital resources have made sharing knowledge, techniques, and experiences easier, fostering a global bonsai community.

Bonsai Exhibitions and Conventions: International bonsai exhibitions and conventions have become significant events, drawing participants from around the world. These events showcase the artistry and skill involved in Bonsai and facilitate cultural exchange and learning among practitioners.

Technological advancements

Technology has profoundly impacted how Bonsai is practiced and appreciated in the modern era.

Online Learning and Virtual Workshops: With the advent of online learning platforms and virtual workshops, access to bonsai education has expanded dramatically. Enthusiasts can learn from master bonsai artists from different parts of the world without leaving their homes.

E-Commerce and Bonsai Trade: The availability of bonsai trees, tools, and supplies has increased with the rise of e-commerce. Enthusiasts can easily purchase rare species, high-quality tools, and specialized bonsai soil from international vendors.

Environmental Consciousness and Sustainability

As awareness of environmental issues grows, Bonsai is increasingly seen through the lens of sustainability and conservation.

Promoting Biodiversity and Conservation: Bonsai can promote biodiversity and the conservation of rare and endangered plant species. By cultivating these species as Bonsai, enthusiasts can contribute to their preservation.

Sustainable Practices: There is a growing emphasis on sustainable practices in bonsai cultivation, including the use of organic fertilizers, pest control methods, and water conservation techniques.

Challenges and opportunities

Despite its growing popularity, Bonsai faces challenges in the modern world, including the preservation of traditional techniques and adapting to changing environmental conditions. However, these challenges also present opportunities for innovation and the continued evolution of Bonsai as an art form.

Preservation of Traditional Techniques: While innovation is vital, there is also a need to preserve traditional bonsai techniques and knowledge. This balance between tradition and innovation is crucial for the art form's integrity and continuity.

Adapting to Climate Change: Climate change poses a significant challenge to bonsai cultivation, affecting growth patterns and pest dynamics. Bonsai practitioners are adapting by selecting more resilient species and modifying care techniques to suit changing environmental conditions.

Youth Engagement: Engaging the younger generation in Bonsai is essential for its future. This involves making Bonsai relevant to younger audiences, possibly through integrating technology, contemporary art forms, and addressing environmental concerns that resonate with them.

Therapeutic and Educational Roles: Bonsai's potential as a therapeutic tool for mental health and as an educational medium in schools and communities is increasingly recognized. These roles could significantly expand the relevance and application of Bonsai in modern society.

In conclusion, Bonsai is a dynamic and evolving art form in the modern world. It bridges the gap between tradition and contemporary practice, intertwines with global cultures, and adapts to the challenges and opportunities of the 21st century. As we continue to nurture and adapt this ancient art, we contribute to its rich tapestry, ensuring its relevance and beauty for future generations.

CHAPTER 2: THE FIRST STEP: CHOOSING YOUR PLANT

Embarking on the bonsai journey begins with a crucial step: choosing the right plant. This chapter is dedicated to guiding you through this initial, yet significant, phase of your bonsai adventure. Selecting a bonsai is not just about finding a tree that appeals to you aesthetically; it involves understanding the compatibility between the plant and its intended environment, recognizing the level of care required, and aligning it with your personal goals and preferences in bonsai cultivation. Whether you are a beginner or looking to expand your collection, this chapter will provide valuable insights into selecting the ideal Bonsai that resonates with your aspirations and thrives in your care.

2.1 Ideal Species For Beginners

Selecting the right species is a crucial first step in your bonsai journey. As a beginner, choosing a species that aligns with your aesthetic preferences and suits your living environment and care capabilities is essential. Here, we explore some ideal species for beginners, highlighting their characteristics and care requirements.

How to Read Bonsai Species Fact Cards

Each bonsai species fact card in this book is designed to give you a quick overview of the key characteristics and care requirements for different bonsai species. Understanding these cards will help you make informed decisions about which species might best suit your bonsai aspirations and conditions. Here's what each section of the card means:

- **Easy to Grow:** This rating gives you an idea of how forgiving the species is, especially for beginners. A higher rating (more stars) means the species is generally easier to care for, making it a good choice for those new to bonsai.

- **Care Requirements:** This indicates the overall effort and specific care needed for the species, including watering, feeding, and pruning. Fewer stars suggest the species is less demanding, while more stars indicate a need for more attentive or specialized care.

- **Pests and Diseases Resistance:** This section assesses the species' resilience to common pests and diseases. More stars mean the species is more resistant, which can lead to easier maintenance and healthier growth.

- **Pruning Difficulty:** This rating reflects how challenging it is to prune the species to achieve desired bonsai shapes. Species with more stars require more skill to prune correctly, making them better suited for experienced practitioners.

- **Indoor/Outdoor Living:** These ratings provide insight into how well the species adapts to indoor or outdoor conditions. More stars indicate a greater suitability for that environment. Some species may thrive indoors, others outdoors, and some can adapt to both with proper care.

- **Water Needs:** This section describes the species' water requirements, ranging from low to high. Understanding the water needs is crucial for maintaining the health and beauty of your bonsai.

    Here is an example of how to read the values in the tables you will encounter later. You also have an example of how to handle the quantities needed duarnte the four seasons

Watering Needs	Spring	Summer	Fall	Winter
Low	1 cup every 10 days	1 cup every 7 days	1 cup every 10 days	1 cup every 14 days
Moderate	1 cup every 7 days	1 cup every 4 days	1 cup every 7 days	1 cup every 10 days
Moderate to High	1 cup every 5 days	1 cup every 3 days	1 cup every 5 days	1 cup every 7 days
High	1 cup every 3 days	1 cup every 2 days	1 cup every 3 days	1 cup every 5 days

- **Temperature Max/Min:** These values give you the maximum and minimum temperature ranges in which the species can thrive. This information is vital for protecting your bonsai from extreme conditions that could harm it.

Disclaimer: Enhancing The Beauty Of Bonsai Through Imagery

As you delve into this chapter and explore the diverse species of bonsai, you will be greeted by a series of images that capture these magnificent trees in their full splendor. We wish to inform you about the nature of these images to enrich your experience as you navigate through this section of the book.

The photographs of bonsai featured in this chapter have undergone artistic enhancement with photo-retouching programs or AI to highlight each species' utmost potential. This process aims to showcase the beauty and distinct qualities of each bonsai variety with exceptional clarity and visual appeal.

It is essential to understand that while these images serve as a beacon of inspiration, showcasing the pinnacle of what can be achieved with dedication and skill, they represent ideals that are the result of extensive care, patience, and time. The journey to attaining such exquisite results is a rewarding endeavor that unfolds over years and is deeply rooted in a commitment to the art and practice of bonsai cultivation.

These enhanced images are intended to inspire and guide your imagination, offering a glimpse into the potential beauty your own bonsai can achieve. They are meant to encourage, not to set expectations for immediate results, reminding us of the artistry and possibilities within bonsai cultivation.

Let this chapter be a source of motivation as you embark on or continue your bonsai journey. Whether you are just starting or have been nurturing bonsai for years, there is always beauty to aspire to and new heights to reach in your practice. May these images inspire you to dream, design, and dedicate yourself to the wonderful art of bonsai, cultivating living sculptures that bring joy and fulfillment for years to come.

Ficus (ficus spp.)

Characteristics: Ficus species are known for their robustness and versatility. They have thick, waxy leaves and often exhibit interesting root structures. Many Ficus varieties can produce aerial roots, adding to their visual appeal.

Care Requirements: Ficus bonsai thrive in warm, humid environments and prefer consistent moisture. They are tolerant of indoor conditions, including lower light and dry air, but they flourish with more humidity and light.

Why Ideal for Beginners: Their resilience to pruning and ability to survive in less-than-ideal conditions make Ficus an excellent choice for those who are still learning the nuances of bonsai care.

Parameter	Rating/Information
Easy to Grow	★★★★★ (5/5)
Care Requirements	★★★☆☆ (3.5/5)
Pests and Diseases Resistance	★★★★☆ (4/5)
Pruning Difficulty	★★★☆☆ (3/5)
Indoor Living	★★★★★ (5/5)
Outdoor Living	★★★☆☆ (3/5)
Water Needs	Moderate to High
Temperature Max	95° / 35°C F
Temperature Min	60°F / 15°C

Bonsai

Leaf detail

Juniper (juniperus spp.)

Characteristics: Junipers are coniferous plants with needle-like leaves. They are known for their hardy nature and the ease with which they can be shaped and trained.

Care Requirements: These trees prefer outdoor settings with plenty of sunlight. They require well-draining soil and moderate watering, being careful not to overwater.

Why Ideal for Beginners: Junipers forgive mistakes, especially in pruning. They are robust and can tolerate a range of outdoor conditions, making them suitable for beginners who want to practice shaping and styling.

Parameter	Rating/Information
Easy to Grow	★★★★☆ (4/5)
Care Requirements	★★★★☆ (4/5)
Pests and Diseases Resistance	★★★☆☆ (3/5)
Pruning Difficulty	★★★★☆ (4/5)
Indoor Living	★★☆☆☆ (2/5)
Outdoor Living	★★★★★ (5/5)
Water Needs	Moderate
Temperature Max	100°F / 38°C
Temperature Min	-10°F / -23°C

Bonsai

Leaf detail

Chinese elm (ulmus parvifolia)

Characteristics: The Chinese Elm boasts small leaves and a fine branch structure, making it visually appealing for Bonsai. It has a smooth, mottled bark that adds to its aesthetic.

Care Requirements: This species is adaptable to both indoor and outdoor environments. It prefers plenty of sunlight and regular watering, adjusting well to the seasonal changes in temperate climates.

Why Ideal for Beginners: The Chinese Elm is a versatile option for novices due to its tolerance for pruning and ability to adapt to various conditions.

Parameter	Rating/Information
Easy to Grow	★★★★☆ (4.5/5)
Care Requirements	★★★★☆ (4/5)
Pests and Diseases Resistance	★★★☆☆ (3/5)
Pruning Difficulty	★★★★☆ (4/5)
Indoor Living	★★★★☆ (4/5)
Outdoor Living	★★★★☆ (4/5)
Water Needs	Moderate
Temperature Max	95° / 35°C F
Temperature Min	15°F / -9°C

Bonsai

Leaf detail

Dwarf schefflera (schefflera arboricola)

Characteristics: This tropical plant, known for its umbrella-shaped leaf clusters, can create an exotic look. It's particularly suited for indoor Bonsai because it prefers warm climates.

Care Requirements: Dwarf Schefflera thrives in indirect but bright light. It's tolerant of irregular watering, making it forgiving for beginners who are still mastering the art of bonsai watering. However, it does prefer a humid environment.

Why Ideal for Beginners: Its resilience to varying indoor conditions and its under- and over-watering tolerance make it a hardy choice for those new to Bonsai. Its rapid growth also allows quicker learning and experimentation with pruning and shaping.

Parameter	Rating/Information
Easy to Grow	★★★★★ (5/5)
Care Requirements	★★★☆☆ (3/5)
Pests and Diseases Resistance	★★★★☆ (4/5)
Pruning Difficulty	★★★☆☆ (3/5)
Indoor Living	★★★★★ (5/5)
Outdoor Living	★★★☆☆ (3/5)
Water Needs	Moderate
Temperature Max	90°F / 32°C
Temperature Min	55°F / 13°C

Bonsai

Leaf detail

In addition to these species, there are other factors to consider when choosing your first Bonsai. Think about your climate, the space where you plan to keep your Bonsai, and how much time you can dedicate to its care. Remember, the best Bonsai for a beginner is one that teaches the fundamentals of bonsai care and brings joy and satisfaction in its cultivation.

As you gain experience and confidence with these beginner-friendly species, you may find yourself drawn to more challenging varieties. Each species offers its own unique learning opportunities and aesthetic qualities, contributing to the diverse and rewarding experience of bonsai cultivation.

2.2 Understanding Climate And Environment

Climate zones and bonsai selection

Different bonsai species thrive in different climate zones. It's essential to understand your local climate zone and choose species that are well-suited to these conditions. Climate zones are categorized based on temperature, humidity, and the length of growing seasons. For instance, a Juniper may thrive in a temperate zone but struggle in a tropical climate.

Temperature and seasonal changes

Like their full-sized counterparts, Bonsai trees are sensitive to temperature changes and often require specific care through the seasons. Some species need a period of dormancy during winter, which is triggered by colder temperatures and shorter daylight hours. In contrast, tropical species may require consistent warmth throughout the year and can be sensitive to low temperatures.

Sunlight and shade requirements

Understanding the light requirements of your Bonsai is crucial. Some species require full sun for most of the day, while others thrive in partial shade. The intensity of light in your area, which can be influenced by latitude and altitude, also plays a role. In regions with intense sunlight, even sun-loving species may need protection during the hottest part of the day.

Humidity and air circulation

Humidity levels can significantly affect the health of your Bonsai. Species from humid environments may struggle in dry climates unless additional humidity is provided. Conversely, trees from arid regions might suffer in a high-humidity climate. Good air circulation is also important for preventing fungal diseases and ensuring the health of your Bonsai.

Soil and water considerations

The type of soil and water availability in your area can influence bonsai cultivation. Some regions have hard water, which can affect soil pH over time. Understanding your local water quality and soil types can guide you in making adjustments to your bonsai care routine, such as using filtered water or specific soil amendments.

Adapting to indoor environments

For those living in urban environments or areas with harsh climates, growing Bonsai indoors might be the only option. Indoor bonsai cultivation requires understanding the limitations and possibilities of your indoor environment, such as light intensity, room temperature, and humidity levels. Species selection becomes even more crucial here, as not all bonsai trees are suited for indoor living.

Local pests and diseases

Every region has its unique set of pests and diseases that can affect plants. Familiarize yourself with common local issues so you can take preventive measures and be prepared to address problems if they arise.

Understanding your local climate and environment is fundamental in bonsai cultivation. It influences everything from species selection to daily care routines. You can create a thriving and sustainable bonsai experience by aligning your bonsai practice with your environment.

2.3 Bonsai Selection Criteria

Standing at the crossroads of selecting your Bonsai is akin to being in a gallery of living art. With its unique form and story, each tree beckons with an unspoken promise of a shared journey. This decision, steeped in both practicality and emotion, is more than just choosing a plant; it's about embarking on a journey of growth, learning, and creative expression.

Imagine each potential Bonsai as a character in a story, with its own past and a future that you will help shape. The older trees, with their gnarled trunks and windswept branches, are like wise sages with tales of resilience and endurance. They speak of years gone by, of seasons weathered, offering a richness of history. Yet, they ask for a caretaker who understands their complex needs and appreciates their mature beauty.

On the other hand, the younger trees, with their supple branches and unmarked trunks, are akin to young adventurers, full of potential and awaiting guidance. They offer a blank canvas, inviting you to imprint your vision and grow alongside them. These trees are not just plants but partners in a creative journey, evolving under your care and attention.

This process of selection is a dance of intuition and insight. It's about listening to that quiet voice within you that resonates with a particular tree. Sometimes, it's a subtle pull, a feeling that this tree, with its unique quirks and features, belongs with you. Other times, it's an instant connection, a sense that your stories are meant to intertwine.

As you make your choice, remember that this Bonsai will become more than just a part of your garden or home. It will become a part of your daily life, a silent companion that shares in your moments of joy, contemplation, and creativity. The right Bonsai will not only fit into your physical space but will also resonate with your spirit, offering a living, breathing canvas for artistic expression and a source of deep, personal fulfillment.

In the end, the Bonsai you choose should be the one that speaks to your heart, aligns with your environment, and calls to your spirit of nurturing and creativity. It's a decision that marks the beginning of an enriching journey that promises to be as rewarding as it is challenging.

2.4 Other Common Bonsai Species

Japanese Maple (Acer palmatum)

Characteristics: Japanese Maple is renowned for its beautiful leaf shapes and colors, especially in autumn. It typically has a graceful, dome-shaped growth habit and can exhibit a range of colors from green to red and purple.

Care-Requirements: Prefers a sunny to partly shaded location with protection from strong afternoon sun. Requires well-draining soil and consistent watering, being careful not to overwater. Sensitive to extreme cold.

Parameter	Information
Easy to Grow	★★★★☆ (4/5)
Care Requirements	★★★★☆ (4/5)
Pests and Diseases Resistance	★★★☆☆ (3/5)
Pruning Difficulty	★★★★☆ (4/5)
Indoor Living	★★☆☆☆ (2/5)
Outdoor Living	★★★★★ (5/5)
Water Needs	Moderate
Temperature Max	85°F / 29°C
Temperature Min	20°F / -7°C

Fukien Tea (Carmona)

Characteristics: Fukien Tea is known for its small, dark green, glossy leaves, and it often produces small white flowers and berries. It has a naturally irregular and somewhat rugged appearance.

Care-Requirements: Requires a warm, humid environment and plenty of light. It's sensitive to temperature changes and prefers stable conditions. Regular watering is essential, but the soil should not be kept overly wet.

Parameter	Information
Easy to Grow	★★★☆☆ (3/5)
Care Requirements	★★★★☆ (4/5)
Pests and Diseases Resistance	★★★☆☆ (3/5)
Pruning Difficulty	★★★☆☆ (3/5)
Indoor Living	★★★★☆ (4/5)
Outdoor Living	★★☆☆☆ (2/5)
Water Needs	Moderate to High
Temperature Max	100°F / 38°C
Temperature Min	40°F / 4°C

Jade Plant (Crassula or portulacaria)

Characteristics: The Jade Plant is a succulent with thick, fleshy leaves and a sturdy trunk, making it an excellent choice for bonsai. It's known for its resilience and ease of care.

Care-Requirements: Prefers bright light and can tolerate direct sunlight. It requires minimal watering, making it a good choice for those new to bonsai. Overwatering can lead to root rot, so allowing the soil to dry out between waterings is crucial.

Parameter	Information
Easy to Grow	★★★★★ (5/5)
Care Requirements	★★★☆☆ (3/5)
Pests and Diseases Resistance	★★★★☆ (4/5)
Pruning Difficulty	★★★☆☆ (3/5)
Indoor Living	★★★★★ (5/5)
Outdoor Living	★★★☆☆ (3/5)
Water Needs	Low
Temperature Max	75°F / 24°C
Temperature Min	50°F / 10°C

Azalea (Rhododendron)

Characteristics: Azaleas, part of the Rhododendron family, are known for their stunning, vibrant flowers and dense foliage. They have a natural tendency to form a compact and rounded shape.

Care-Requirements: Prefers acidic soil and partial shade. Regular watering is essential, especially during the flowering period, but ensure good drainage to avoid root rot. They require protection from extreme cold.

Parameter	Information
Easy to Grow	★★★☆☆ (3/5)
Care Requirements	★★★★☆ (4/5)
Pests and Diseases Resistance	★★★☆☆ (3/5)
Pruning Difficulty	★★★☆☆ (3/5)
Indoor Living	★★☆☆☆ (2/5)
Outdoor Living	★★★★☆ (4/5)
Water Needs	Moderate
Temperature Max	80°F / 27°C
Temperature Min	30°F / -1°C

Bougainvillea

Characteristics: Bougainvillea is celebrated for its lush growth and vibrant, colorful bracts that surround its flowers. It's a fast-growing and hardy plant, ideal for creating a striking bonsai.

Care-Requirements: Thrives in full sun and requires well-draining soil. It's drought-tolerant but responds well to regular watering during the growing season. Pruning is essential to control its rapid growth and encourage flowering.

Parameter	Information
Easy to Grow	★★★★☆ (4/5)
Care Requirements	★★★☆☆ (3/5)
Pests and Diseases Resistance	★★★★☆ (4/5)
Pruning Difficulty	★★★★☆ (4/5)
Indoor Living	★☆☆☆☆ (1/5)
Outdoor Living	★★★★★ (5/5)
Water Needs	Moderate
Temperature Max	100°F / 38°C
Temperature Min	30°F / -1°C

Serissa (Serissa Foetida)

Characteristics: Often called the "Snow Rose" or "Thousand Stars," Serissa is known for its tiny leaves and profuse, star-shaped flowers. It's a popular choice for bonsai due to its compact growth and flowering habit.

Care-Requirements: Prefers consistent moisture and good lighting. It can be sensitive to changes in temperature and watering, so maintaining a stable environment is key. Benefits from regular pruning and pinching to maintain shape and encourage flowering.

Parameter	Information
Easy to Grow	★★★☆☆ (3/5)
Care Requirements	★★★★☆ (4/5)
Pests and Diseases Resistance	★★★☆☆ (3/5)
Pruning Difficulty	★★★☆☆ (3/5)
Indoor Living	★★★☆☆ (3/5)
Outdoor Living	★★★☆☆ (3/5)
Water Needs	Moderate to High
Temperature Max	85°F / 29°C
Temperature Min	40°F / 4°C

Boxwood (Buxus)

Characteristics: Boxwood is known for its dense foliage and small, glossy leaves. It's a hardy species, often used for classic bonsai shapes due to its ease of training and pruning.

Care-Requirements: Prefers partial shade to full sun and requires well-draining soil. Regular watering is important, but avoid waterlogging. Boxwood is adaptable but benefits from protection during extreme cold.

Parameter	Information
Easy to Grow	★★★★☆ (4/5)
Care Requirements	★★★☆☆ (3/5)
Pests and Diseases Resistance	★★★☆☆ (3/5)
Pruning Difficulty	★★★☆☆ (3/5)
Indoor Living	★☆☆☆☆ (1/5)
Outdoor Living	★★★★★ (5/5)
Water Needs	Moderate
Temperature Max	95°F / 35°C
Temperature Min	20°F / -7°C

Chinese Sweet Plum (Sageretia Theezans)

Characteristics: The Chinese Sweet Plum is admired for its attractive bark, small leaves, and tiny white flowers. It's known for its fast growth and can produce small, plum-like fruits.

Care-Requirements: Thrives in bright, indirect light and requires a humid environment. Regular watering is essential, but ensure good drainage. It's sensitive to cold and needs protection in winter.

Parameter	Information
Easy to Grow	★★★☆☆ (3/5)
Care Requirements	★★★★☆ (4/5)
Pests and Diseases Resistance	★★★☆☆ (3/5)
Pruning Difficulty	★★★☆☆ (3/5)
Indoor Living	★★★★☆ (4/5)
Outdoor Living	★★☆☆☆ (2/5)
Water Needs	Moderate to High
Temperature Max	90°F / 32°C
Temperature Min	50°F / 10°C

Olive Tree (Olea Europaea)

Characteristics: The Olive Tree is cherished for its gnarled trunk, silvery leaves, and the ability to produce olives. It's a symbol of peace and longevity, making it a meaningful choice for bonsai.

Care-Requirements: Prefers full sun and well-draining soil. It's drought-tolerant but benefits from regular watering during the growing season. Tolerates a range of temperatures but should be protected from severe frost.

Parameter	Information
Easy to Grow	★★★★☆ (4/5)
Care Requirements	★★★☆☆ (3/5)
Pests and Diseases Resistance	★★★★☆ (4/5)
Pruning Difficulty	★★★☆☆ (3/5)
Indoor Living	★★☆☆☆ (2/5)
Outdoor Living	★★★★★ (5/5)
Water Needs	Low to Moderate
Temperature Max	100°F / 38°C
Temperature Min	20°F / -7°C

Money Tree (Pachira Aquatica)

Characteristics: The Money Tree is known for its braided trunk and lush, green leaves. It's popular for its ornamental value and is believed to bring good luck and fortune.

Care-Requirements: Prefers bright, indirect light and a humid environment. It's important to keep the soil consistently moist but not waterlogged. The Money Tree is sensitive to overwatering, which can lead to root rot.

Parameter	Information
Easy to Grow	★★★★☆ (4/5)
Care Requirements	★★★☆☆ (3/5)
Pests and Diseases Resistance	★★★☆☆ (3/5)
Pruning Difficulty	★★★☆☆ (3/5)
Indoor Living	★★★★★ (5/5)
Outdoor Living	★★☆☆☆ (2/5)
Water Needs	Moderate
Temperature Max	90°F / 32°C
Temperature Min	50°F / 10°C

Privet (Ligustrum)

Characteristics: Privet is favored for bonsai due to its small leaves, dense foliage, and fast growth. It's versatile for various bonsai styles and can produce white flowers followed by black berries.

Care-Requirements: Thrives in full sun to partial shade. Regular pruning is needed to maintain shape and encourage branching. It's adaptable to various soil types but requires consistent moisture.

Parameter	Information
Easy to Grow	★★★★☆ (4/5)
Care Requirements	★★★☆☆ (3/5)
Pests and Diseases Resistance	★★★☆☆ (3/5)
Pruning Difficulty	★★★☆☆ (3/5)
Indoor Living	★☆☆☆☆ (1/5)
Outdoor Living	★★★★★ (5/5)
Water Needs	Moderate
Temperature Max	95°F / 35°C
Temperature Min	20°F / -7°C

Cotoneaster

Characteristics: Cotoneaster is known for its small, glossy leaves, pink flowers, and red berries. It's a hardy plant that adapts well to bonsai cultivation, offering year-round interest.

Care-Requirements: Prefers full sun for best flowering and fruiting. Requires well-draining soil and moderate watering. It's frost-hardy but benefits from some protection in extreme cold.

Parameter	Information
Easy to Grow	★★★★☆ (4/5)
Care Requirements	★★★☆☆ (3/5)
Pests and Diseases Resistance	★★★★☆ (4/5)
Pruning Difficulty	★★★☆☆ (3/5)
Indoor Living	★☆☆☆☆ (1/5)
Outdoor Living	★★★★★ (5/5)
Water Needs	Moderate
Temperature Max	90°F / 32°C
Temperature Min	15°F / -9°C

Lemon and Orange Trees (Citrus Limon and Sinensis)

Characteristics: Citrus trees like Lemon (C. Limon) and Orange (C. Sinensis) are prized for their fragrant flowers, glossy leaves, and ability to produce fruit. They add a Mediterranean touch to bonsai collections.

Care-Requirements: These trees thrive in full sun and require well-draining soil. They need regular watering but are sensitive to overwatering. Citrus trees prefer a consistent and warm climate.

Parameter	Information
Easy to Grow	★★★☆☆ (3/5)
Care Requirements	★★★★☆ (4/5)
Pests and Diseases Resistance	★★★☆☆ (3/5)
Pruning Difficulty	★★★☆☆ (3/5)
Indoor Living	★★★☆☆ (3/5)
Outdoor Living	★★★★☆ (4/5)
Water Needs	Moderate
Temperature Max	95°F / 35°C
Temperature Min	50°F / 10°C

Brazilian Rain Tree (Pithecellobium tortum)

Characteristics: Known for its twisting trunk and delicate, fern-like foliage, the Brazilian Rain Tree is a popular choice for bonsai. It's particularly noted for its responsiveness to light, with leaves that close at night.

Care-Requirements: Prefers bright, indirect light or partial sun. Requires regular watering and high humidity. It's sensitive to cold temperatures and needs protection during winter.

Parameter	Information
Easy to Grow	★★★☆☆ (3/5)
Care Requirements	★★★★☆ (4/5)
Pests and Diseases Resistance	★★★☆☆ (3/5)
Pruning Difficulty	★★★☆☆ (3/5)
Indoor Living	★★★★☆ (4/5)
Outdoor Living	★★★☆☆ (3/5)
Water Needs	High
Temperature Max	90°F / 32°C
Temperature Min	55°F / 13°C

Brush Cerry (Eugenia myrtifolia and syzygium)

Characteristics: These species are known for their small, glossy leaves, and Syzygium also produces attractive flowers and edible fruit. They are versatile for various bonsai styles.

Care-Requirements: Prefers full sun to partial shade. Regular watering is important, but the soil should not be waterlogged. They are fairly adaptable but benefit from protection in freezing temperatures.

Parameter	Information
Easy to Grow	★★★★☆ (4/5)
Care Requirements	★★★☆☆ (3/5)
Pests and Diseases Resistance	★★★☆☆ (3/5)
Pruning Difficulty	★★★☆☆ (3/5)
Indoor Living	★★★☆☆ (3/5)
Outdoor Living	★★★★☆ (4/5)
Water Needs	Moderate
Temperature Max	95°F / 35°C
Temperature Min	30°F / -1°C

Fuchsia

Characteristics: Fuchsia is known for its beautiful, pendulous flowers and dark green leaves. It's a popular choice for bonsai due to its unique floral display and graceful growth.

Care-Requirements: Prefers cooler conditions and partial shade. Requires consistently moist soil and good air circulation. Fuchsia is sensitive to high heat and dry conditions.

Parameter	Information
Easy to Grow	★★★☆☆ (3/5)
Care Requirements	★★★★☆ (4/5)
Pests and Diseases Resistance	★★★☆☆ (3/5)
Pruning Difficulty	★★★☆☆ (3/5)
Indoor Living	★★★★☆ (4/5)
Outdoor Living	★★★☆☆ (3/5)
Water Needs	High
Temperature Max	75°F / 24°C
Temperature Min	40°F / 4°C

Japanese Holly (Ilex Crenata)

Characteristics: Japanese Holly is favored for its small, glossy leaves and compact growth habit. It's often used for creating formal bonsai styles and can produce small, black berries.

Care-Requirements: Thrives in full sun to partial shade. Prefers well-draining soil and regular watering, but is tolerant of a range of soil conditions. It's quite hardy but benefits from protection from extreme cold.

Parameter	Information
Easy to Grow	★★★★☆ (4/5)
Care Requirements	★★★☆☆ (3/5)
Pests and Diseases Resistance	★★★★☆ (4/5)
Pruning Difficulty	★★★☆☆ (3/5)
Indoor Living	★☆☆☆☆ (1/5)
Outdoor Living	★★★★★ (5/5)
Water Needs	Moderate
Temperature Max	90°F / 32°C
Temperature Min	20°F / -7°C

Premna

Characteristics: Premna is known for its rapid growth, small leaves, and robust trunk. It's highly valued in bonsai for its adaptability to various styles and ability to quickly develop an aged appearance.

Care-Requirements: Prefers a warm climate and full sun. Requires regular watering and well-draining soil. Premna is relatively hardy but should be protected from frost.

Parameter	Information
Easy to Grow	★★★★☆ (4/5)
Care Requirements	★★★☆☆ (3/5)
Pests and Diseases Resistance	★★★☆☆ (3/5)
Pruning Difficulty	★★★☆☆ (3/5)
Indoor Living	★★★☆☆ (3/5)
Outdoor Living	★★★★☆ (4/5)
Water Needs	Moderate
Temperature Max	100°F / 38°C
Temperature Min	40°F / 4°C

Gardenia

Characteristics: Gardenia is celebrated for its fragrant white flowers and glossy, dark green leaves. It's a popular choice for bonsai due to its beautiful blooms and elegant appearance.

Care-Requirements: Prefers bright, indirect light and high humidity. Requires well-draining, acidic soil and consistent moisture. Gardenias are sensitive to temperature changes and need protection from extreme cold.

Parameter	Information
Easy to Grow	★★★☆☆ (3/5)
Care Requirements	★★★★☆ (4/5)
Pests and Diseases Resistance	★★★☆☆ (3/5)
Pruning Difficulty	★★★☆☆ (3/5)
Indoor Living	★★★☆☆ (3/5)
Outdoor Living	★★★☆☆ (3/5)
Water Needs	Moderate to High
Temperature Max	85°F / 29°C
Temperature Min	60°F / 14°C

Crape Myrtle (Lagerstroemia Indica)

Characteristics: Crape Myrtle is known for its showy flowers, attractive bark, and long blooming period. It's a favored species for bonsai due to its colorful display and graceful branching.

Care-Requirements: Thrives in full sun and requires well-draining soil. It's drought-tolerant but benefits from regular watering during the growing season. Crape Myrtle is relatively hardy but should be protected from harsh winter conditions.

Parameter	Information
Easy to Grow	★★★★☆ (4/5)
Care Requirements	★★★☆☆ (3/5)
Pests and Diseases Resistance	★★★★☆ (4/5)
Pruning Difficulty	★★★☆☆ (3/5)
Indoor Living	★☆☆☆☆ (1/5)
Outdoor Living	★★★★★ (5/5)
Water Needs	Moderate
Temperature Max	95°F / 35°C
Temperature Min	20°F / -7°C

Common Myrtle (Myrtus Communis)

Characteristics: Common Myrtle is admired for its aromatic foliage, star-shaped white flowers, and blue-black berries. It's a classic choice for bonsai, offering year-round interest and a pleasant fragrance.

Care-Requirements: Prefers full sun to partial shade and well-draining soil. Regular watering is important, but the soil should not be waterlogged. Myrtle is quite hardy but benefits from protection in freezing temperatures.

Parameter	Information
Easy to Grow	★★★★☆ (4/5)
Care Requirements	★★★☆☆ (3/5)
Pests and Diseases Resistance	★★★★☆ (4/5)
Pruning Difficulty	★★★☆☆ (3/5)
Indoor Living	★★☆☆☆ (2/5)
Outdoor Living	★★★★★ (5/5)
Water Needs	Moderate
Temperature Max	90°F / 32°C
Temperature Min	30°F / -1°C

Pyracantha

Characteristics: Pyracantha, known for its vibrant berries and thorny branches, is a popular bonsai choice. It offers year-round interest with white flowers in spring and bright berries in fall and winter.

Care-Requirements: Prefers full sun to partial shade. Requires well-draining soil and regular watering, but is drought-tolerant once established. Pruning is essential to maintain shape and encourage berry production.

Parameter	Information
Easy to Grow	★★★★☆ (4/5)
Care Requirements	★★★☆☆ (3/5)
Pests and Diseases Resistance	★★★☆☆ (3/5)
Pruning Difficulty	★★★☆☆ (3/5)
Indoor Living	★☆☆☆☆ (1/5)
Outdoor Living	★★★★★ (5/5)
Water Needs	Moderate
Temperature Max	95°F / 35°C
Temperature Min	20°F / -7°C

Water Jasmine (Wrightia Religiosa)

Characteristics: Wrightia religiosa is known for its delicate, fragrant white flowers and fine foliage. It's a favorite in bonsai for its flowering habit and elegant form.

Care-Requirements: Prefers bright, indirect light and high humidity. Requires consistent moisture and well-draining soil. It's sensitive to cold and needs protection during cooler months.

Parameter	Information
Easy to Grow	★★★☆☆ (3/5)
Care Requirements	★★★★☆ (4/5)
Pests and Diseases Resistance	★★★☆☆ (3/5)
Pruning Difficulty	★★★☆☆ (3/5)
Indoor Living	★★★★☆ (4/5)
Outdoor Living	★★★☆☆ (3/5)
Water Needs	High
Temperature Max	90°F / 32°C
Temperature Min	55°F / 13°C

Acacia

Characteristics: Acacias are known for their feathery foliage and striking yellow flowers. They are fast-growing and can add a touch of the exotic to a bonsai collection.

Care-Requirements: Prefers full sun and well-draining soil. They are drought-resistant but benefit from regular watering during the growing season. Acacias can be sensitive to cold and may require protection in cooler climates.

Parameter	Information
Easy to Grow	★★★★☆ (4/5)
Care Requirements	★★★☆☆ (3/5)
Pests and Diseases Resistance	★★★☆☆ (3/5)
Pruning Difficulty	★★★★☆ (4/5)
Indoor Living	★☆☆☆☆ (1/5)
Outdoor Living	★★★★☆ (4/5)
Water Needs	Low to Moderate
Temperature Max	100°F / 38°C
Temperature Min	30°F/-1°C

Camellia

Characteristics: Camellias are admired for their glossy, dark green leaves and stunning flowers, which come in a range of colors. They are a symbol of elegance and refinement in the bonsai world.

Care-Requirements: Prefers partial shade and protection from strong afternoon sun. Requires acidic, well-draining soil and consistent moisture. Camellias are sensitive to overwatering and extreme cold.

Parameter	Information
Easy to Grow	★★★☆☆ (3/5)
Care Requirements	★★★★☆ (4/5)
Pests and Diseases Resistance	★★★☆☆ (3/5)
Pruning Difficulty	★★★☆☆ (3/5)
Indoor Living	★★☆☆☆ (2/5)
Outdoor Living	★★★★☆ (4/5)
Water Needs	Moderate
Temperature Max	80°F / 27°C
Temperature Min	30°F / -1°C

Bamboo (Bambusoideae)

Characteristics: Bamboo is unique in bonsai for its fast growth and distinctive, hollow stems. It's known for its simplicity and elegance.

Care-Requirements: Thrives in bright, indirect light and prefers a humid environment. Bamboo requires regular watering and well-draining soil. It's adaptable to temperature variations but benefits from protection against harsh conditions.

Parameter	Information
Easy to Grow	★★★★★ (5/5)
Care Requirements	★★★☆☆ (3/5)
Pests and Diseases Resistance	★★★★☆ (4/5)
Pruning Difficulty	★★☆☆☆ (2/5)
Indoor Living	★★★★☆ (4/5)
Outdoor Living	★★★☆☆ (3/5)
Water Needs	High
Temperature Max	90°F / 32°C
Temperature Min	50°F / 10°C

Hibiscus

Characteristics: Hibiscus is known for its large, colorful flowers and glossy leaves. It adds a tropical flair to bonsai collections and can bloom year-round in the right conditions.

Care-Requirements: Prefers full sun and well-draining soil. Regular watering is essential, but the soil should not be waterlogged. Hibiscus is sensitive to cold and needs protection in cooler climates.

Parameter	Information
Easy to Grow	★★★☆☆ (3/5)
Care Requirements	★★★☆☆ (3/5)
Pests and Diseases Resistance	★★★☆☆ (3/5)
Pruning Difficulty	★★★☆☆ (3/5)
Indoor Living	★★☆☆☆ (2/5)
Outdoor Living	★★★★☆ (4/5)
Water Needs	Moderate to High
Temperature Max	95°F / 35°C
Temperature Min	50°F / 10°C

Eucalyptus

Characteristics: Eucalyptus is known for its aromatic leaves and rapid growth. It's a unique choice for bonsai, offering an interesting peeling bark and a refreshing scent.

Care-Requirements: Prefers full sun and well-draining soil. It's drought-tolerant but benefits from regular watering during the growing season. Eucalyptus is sensitive to cold and should be protected from frost.

Parameter	Information
Easy to Grow	★★★★☆ (4/5)
Care Requirements	★★★☆☆ (3/5)
Pests and Diseases Resistance	★★★☆☆ (3/5)
Pruning Difficulty	★★★★☆ (4/5)
Indoor Living	★☆☆☆☆ (1/5)
Outdoor Living	★★★★★ (5/5)
Water Needs	Moderate
Temperature Max	100°F / 38°C
Temperature Min	30°F / -1°C

Lilac (Syringa)

Characteristics: Lilacs are valued for their fragrant flowers and heart-shaped leaves. They offer a stunning floral display, typically in shades of purple and white.

Care-Requirements: Prefers full sun and well-draining, slightly alkaline soil. Regular watering is important, especially during blooming. Lilacs require a period of winter chill for optimal flowering.

Parameter	Information
Easy to Grow	★★★☆☆ (3/5)
Care Requirements	★★★★☆ (4/5)
Pests and Diseases Resistance	★★★☆☆ (3/5)
Pruning Difficulty	★★★☆☆ (3/5)
Indoor Living	★☆☆☆☆ (1/5)
Outdoor Living	★★★★☆ (4/5)
Water Needs	Moderate
Temperature Max	85°F / 29°C
Temperature Min	-10°F / -23°C

Ming aralia (Polyscias Fruticosa)

Characteristics: Ming Aralia is known for its finely divided leaves and woody stems. It's an elegant plant, often used for indoor bonsai due to its adaptability to lower light conditions.

Care-Requirements: Prefers bright, indirect light and high humidity. Requires well-draining soil and consistent moisture. Sensitive to overwatering and cold drafts.

Parameter	Information
Easy to Grow	★★★☆☆ (3/5)
Care Requirements	★★★★☆ (4/5)
Pests and Diseases Resistance	★★★☆☆ (3/5)
Pruning Difficulty	★★★☆☆ (3/5)
Indoor Living	★★★★★ (5/5)
Outdoor Living	★★☆☆☆ (2/5)
Water Needs	Moderate
Temperature Max	80°F / 27°C
Temperature Min	60°F / 15°C

Rosemary (Rosemarinus)

Characteristics: Rosemary is a popular herb known for its needle-like leaves and fragrant aroma. It's a hardy plant, often used in bonsai for its attractive growth habit and ability to be shaped.

Care-Requirements: Prefers full sun and well-draining soil. It's drought-tolerant and requires minimal watering. Rosemary can be sensitive to overwatering and extreme cold.

Parameter	Information
Easy to Grow	★★★★★ (5/5)
Care Requirements	★★★☆☆ (3/5)
Pests and Diseases Resistance	★★★★☆ (4/5)
Pruning Difficulty	★★★☆☆ (3/5)
Indoor Living	★★★☆☆ (3/5)
Outdoor Living	★★★★★ (5/5)
Water Needs	Low
Temperature Max	90°F / 32°C
Temperature Min	30°F / -1°C

CHAPTER 3: WATER: THE ELIXIR OF LIFE FOR BONSAI

Water, often referred to as the elixir of life, plays a pivotal role in the art and science of Bonsai. In Chapter 4, we delve into the intricate world of watering, a fundamental aspect that can make or break the health of your miniature tree. This chapter is dedicated to exploring the various facets of watering, offering insights into how this simple yet crucial element can be harnessed to nurture and sustain your Bonsai.

Watering a bonsai is not just a routine task; it's an art that requires understanding, observation, and a deep connection with your tree. The right watering technique can promote vigorous health, lush foliage, and can significantly impact the overall development of your Bonsai. Conversely, improper watering is one of the most common causes of issues in bonsai care.

In this chapter, we will explore the nuances of watering, from understanding the unique needs of different bonsai species to mastering the techniques that ensure your tree receives the optimal amount of moisture. We'll discuss how to assess when a bonsai needs water, the best methods for watering, and how to adjust your watering routine to accommodate changes in the environment and the tree's growth cycle.

Whether you are a beginner just starting to understand the basics or an experienced practitioner looking to refine your skills, this chapter will provide valuable guidance on one of the most essential aspects of bonsai care. Through a deeper understanding of watering, you can ensure that your Bonsai not only survives but thrives, showcasing the beauty and resilience of these living sculptures.

3.1 Irrigation Techniques

Irrigation, or the process of watering bonsai, is a skill that lies at the heart of successful bonsai cultivation. This section explores various techniques and approaches to ensure your Bonsai receives the right amount of water, delivered in a way that promotes its health and vitality.

Understanding your bonsai's water needs

Species-Specific Requirements: Different bonsai species have varying water needs. Some species prefer consistently moist soil, while others thrive in slightly drier conditions. Understanding the specific requirements of your bonsai species is crucial.

Observing Soil Moisture: Learning to assess soil moisture is key. This can be done through visual inspection, feeling the soil's top layer, or using tools like moisture meters. The goal is to water the tree when the soil begins to dry out, but before it becomes completely dry.

Watering techniques

Top Watering: This is the most common method, where water is poured over the top of the soil using a watering can with a fine nozzle. This method allows for even distribution of water, ensuring that the entire root system is adequately moistened.

Bottom Watering: In this method, the bonsai pot is placed in a tray of water, allowing the soil to absorb moisture from the bottom up. This can be effective for ensuring deep watering, but care must be taken not to leave the Bonsai in water for too long to avoid root rot.

Misting: While misting does not replace regular watering, it can be beneficial for maintaining humidity around the Bonsai, especially for species that thrive in more humid environments. Misting can also help clean the leaves and improve the tree's ability to photosynthesize.

Frequency and timing of watering

Regular Monitoring: There is no one-size-fits-all schedule for watering Bonsai. The frequency depends on various factors including the species, size of the tree and pot, soil composition, and environmental conditions. Regular monitoring is essential to determine when watering is needed.

easonal Adjustments: Watering routines need to be adjusted according to the seasons. During the growing season (spring and summer), Bonsai may require more frequent watering, while in the dormant season (fall and winter), the need for water typically decreases.

Water quality

Considerations: The quality of water used can affect the health of the Bonsai. Some species may be sensitive to chemicals commonly found in tap water. Using rainwater or filtered water can sometimes be beneficial.

pH Levels: The pH level of water can also impact the soil and, consequently, the health of the Bonsai. Knowing the preferred pH level for your bonsai species and testing your water can help in maintaining the right soil conditions.

Avoiding common watering mistakes

Overwatering and Underwatering: Both can be detrimental to bonsai health. Overwatering can lead to root rot and fungal diseases, while under-watering can cause the tree to dry out and weaken.

Uneven Watering: Ensuring that the entire root ball is evenly moistened is important for the overall health of the tree. Uneven watering can lead to dry spots or overly wet areas in the soil.

3.2 Managing Humidity And Dryness

The balance of humidity and dryness is crucial for the health of a bonsai tree. This section explores how to manage these environmental factors to create an ideal growing condition for your Bonsai.

Understanding the role of humidity

Importance for Bonsai: Humidity plays a significant role in the overall health of a bonsai. It affects transpiration rates and can impact the tree's ability to absorb water and nutrients of Bonsai, particularly tropical varieties, require higher humidity levels to thrive, while others are more tolerant of dry air.

Creating a Humid Microclimate: For indoor Bonsai or those in dry climates, creating a humid microclimate can be beneficial. This can be achieved by placing the Bonsai on a humidity tray filled with water and pebbles, ensuring that the pot is not sitting directly in water. Misting the foliage can also help, though it should not be relied upon as the sole source of humidity.

Dealing with dry air

Challenges: Dry air, especially in heated indoor environments during winter, can pose a challenge to maintaining bonsai health. It can lead to rapid soil moisture loss and increased transpiration stress on the tree.

Strategies to Increase Humidity: Besides using a humidity tray, grouping plants together can help increase the local humidity. Using a room humidifier can also be effective, especially in very dry indoor environments.

Monitoring and adjusting

Regular Observation: Keeping a close eye on your Bonsai and its environment is key. Look for signs of stress due to low humidity, such as browning leaf tips or a general dull appearance of the foliage.

Adjustments: Be prepared to adjust your watering and humidity management strategies in response to changes in the environment, such as the onset of winter or a heatwave in summer.

3.3 Common Signs Of Watering Issues

Watering is a critical aspect of bonsai care, and understanding the signs of improper watering is essential for maintaining the health of your tree. This subchapter delves into the common indicators of both overwatering and under-watering, providing insights into how to identify and address these issues effectively.

Identifying overwatering

Overwatering is a common issue in bonsai care, often stemming from a well-intentioned desire to ensure the tree doesn't dry out. However, too much water can lead to several problems:

Yellowing Leaves: An early sign of overwatering is the yellowing of leaves. Unlike the natural yellowing that occurs in some species during certain seasons, this is often a uniform discoloration and may be accompanied by leaf drop. It's a sign that the roots are struggling to function properly due to excess moisture.

Root Rot: The most severe consequence of overwatering is root rot. This occurs when excess water suffocates the roots, depriving them of oxygen and creating an environment conducive to harmful fungi. The roots may become soft, brown, and mushy. Unfortunately, root rot can be fatal if not addressed promptly.

Mold and Fungus Growth: Overly moist conditions can also encourage the growth of mold and fungus in the soil and on the tree. This not only detracts from the aesthetic appeal of the Bonsai but can also be harmful to its health.

Recognizing under-watering

Under-watering, on the other hand, can be just as detrimental to bonsai health, often resulting from fear of overwatering or neglect. Recognizing the signs of insufficient watering is crucial for the timely intervention:

Dry, Crispy Leaves: One of the most obvious signs of under-watering is when the leaves become dry and brittle. They may lose their lush green color, turning a dull shade, and feel crispy to the touch. This is a clear indication that the tree is not receiving enough moisture.

Wilting: A bonsai suffering from lack of water may exhibit wilting, where the leaves and branches droop noticeably. This is the tree's response to insufficient moisture, as it tries to reduce the surface area exposed to the air to conserve water.

Soil Pulling Away from the Pot: When the soil becomes extremely dry, it can start to pull away from the sides of the pot. This is a sign that the soil has been dry for an extended period and that the tree is likely under significant water stress.

Responsive watering practices

Addressing watering issues requires a responsive and attentive approach:

Adjusting Watering Routines: If you notice signs of overwatering, allow the soil to dry out more between waterings and ensure that the pot has adequate drainage. For under-watered trees, gradually increase watering frequency. It might be necessary to soak the pot in water briefly to thoroughly rehydrate the soil.

Monitoring and Adaptation: Regularly monitor the moisture level of the soil using tactile or visual cues, or moisture meters. Be prepared to adapt your watering practices to changes in the environment, such as temperature fluctuations, changes in humidity, and the tree's growth cycle.

Recovery and Care: Trees that have been overwatered or under-watered will need careful attention as they recover. Adjust your care routine to support their recovery, which may include modifying light exposure, fertilization, and other aspects of care.

Understanding the signs of watering issues and responding appropriately is key to successful bonsai cultivation. By being attentive to the needs of your Bonsai and adjusting your watering practices accordingly, you can ensure that your tree remains healthy and vibrant, reflecting this art form's unique beauty and resilience.

CHAPTER 4: LIGHT AND SHADOW: POSITIONING YOUR BONSAI

Chapter 7, "Light and Shadow: Positioning Your Bonsai," delves into the crucial role of light in bonsai care and aesthetics. Understanding how light affects growth, health, and the visual appeal of your Bonsai is essential, whether you're growing your tree indoors or outdoors.

In this chapter, we'll explore how different bonsai species react

to various light conditions and how to position your Bonsai to receive the optimal amount of light. We'll discuss the artistic aspects of using light and shadow to enhance the visual impact of your Bonsai, creating depth and highlighting its best features.

Additionally, we'll address practical solutions for common lighting challenges, such as using artificial lights for indoor Bonsai and protecting trees from intense sunlight. By the end of this chapter, you'll have a comprehensive understanding of how to effectively use light to maintain your Bonsai's health and elevate its beauty.

4.1 Light Requirements For Different Species

Light, an essential element for all plants, plays a particularly nuanced role in the world of Bonsai. Each species of Bonsai has its unique light requirements, which can significantly influence its health, growth, and appearance. Understanding these requirements is key to providing the best care for your Bonsai, regardless of its type.

General light requirements in bonsai

Full Sun Species: Many bonsai trees, especially those native to sunny, dry climates, thrive in full sun. They require several hours of direct sunlight each day to maintain their health and vigor.

Partial Shade Species: Some bonsai prefer partial shade, where they receive a mix of sunlight and shade throughout the day. This is often true for species that naturally grow in forested or shaded areas.

Shade-Tolerant Species: There are also Bonsai that can thrive in low-light conditions, although this is less common. These species are typically adapted to grow in understory environments in nature.

Light requirements for specific bonsai species

Let's consider the four species mentioned in Chapter 3 and how their light requirements impact their care:

Ficus Bonsai: Ficus bonsai generally prefer bright, indirect light as a tropical species. They can tolerate some direct sunlight, but they benefit from afternoon shade in very hot climates to prevent leaf scorch.

Juniper Bonsai: Junipers are sun-loving plants and require full sun to develop their best color and compact growth habit. Insufficient sunlight can lead to leggy growth and a decrease in foliage density.

Chinese Elm Bonsai: Chinese Elms are versatile in their light needs. They can tolerate full sun but also do well in partial shade, making them suitable for a variety of growing conditions.

Dwarf Schefflera Bonsai: The Dwarf Schefflera, being a tropical plant, prefers bright, indirect light. It can adapt to lower light conditions better than many other bonsai species, but too little light will impede its growth.

Practical examples

Ficus in an Apartment: A Ficus bonsai in an apartment setting can be placed near a south-facing window where it receives plenty of indirect sunlight. If the light is too intense, a sheer curtain can be used to diffuse it.

Juniper in a Garden: A Juniper bonsai in a garden should be positioned where it can bask in full sunlight for most of the day. This exposure is crucial for the tree to maintain its compact foliage and characteristic coloration.

Chinese Elm on a Patio: A spot that receives morning sun and afternoon shade would be ideal for a Chinese Elm on a patio, especially in regions with hot summers.

Dwarf Schefflera in an Office: This Bonsai can thrive in an office environment with fluorescent lighting as long as it's placed in a location where it receives adequate ambient light.

Understanding and meeting the light requirements of your bonsai species is crucial for their health and aesthetic appeal. Each species has its preferences, and by tailoring the light exposure to these needs, you can ensure your Bonsai thrives and displays its full beauty.

4.2 Best Practices For Placement

The placement of a bonsai, a decision that intertwines the art of aesthetics with the science of horticulture, is a thoughtful process that significantly impacts the health and beauty of these miniature trees.

When contemplating the placement of your Bonsai, envision it not just as a plant in a pot but as a living sculpture interacting with its surroundings. The location where you place your Bonsai can dramatically affect its growth, shape, and even its coloration.

Consider the journey of sunlight throughout the day and how it interacts with your space. A bonsai placed in a spot that catches the gentle morning sun can bask in its warmth without the risk of the harsh afternoon rays that might scorch its leaves. This dance with the sun is not just about providing light; it's about creating a rhythm for your Bonsai that mimics its natural environment.

In addition to light, think about the air movement around your Bonsai. Good air circulation is vital for the health of the tree, helping to prevent fungal diseases and encouraging robust growth. However, too much wind can dry out the Bonsai quickly, especially smaller ones with limited soil volume. Finding a balance, where your Bonsai receives a gentle breeze, yet is shielded from harsh winds, is like finding the perfect spot where it can breathe and flourish without stress.

The seasonal changes also play a crucial role in the placement of your Bonsai. During the warmer months, your Bonsai might relish being outdoors, soaking in the natural environment. Yet, as the colder season approaches, considerations change. Some bonsai, particularly those from temperate regions, require a period of dormancy and can withstand cold temperatures. Others, especially tropical varieties, need protection from the frost and may thrive better indoors during winter.

Indoor placement comes with its own set of challenges and opportunities. Here, you're creating an artificial environment that needs to mimic the natural conditions as closely as possible. Factors like room temperature, humidity, and proximity to artificial heat sources or air conditioning play a significant role. Placing a bonsai near a window where it can receive ample natural light might be ideal, but beware of cold drafts or excessive heat from radiators. Sometimes, supplementing with artificial grow lights is necessary to provide adequate light, especially in darker winter.

The aesthetic aspect of placement also cannot be overlooked. The spot you choose for your Bonsai should cater to its physical needs and display its beauty to its best advantage. A well-placed bonsai becomes a focal point, drawing the eye and inviting contemplation. It should be positioned at a height where its details can be appreciated, perhaps on a stand or table, where its form and structure can be viewed comfortably.

In essence, the placement of your Bonsai is a harmonious blend of catering to its physical needs and showcasing its natural beauty. It's about understanding and respecting the tree's requirements while allowing it to express its character and charm. Through thoughtful placement, your Bonsai becomes not just a plant in your care, but a living piece of art in your space, bringing with it a sense of peace and natural beauty.

4.3 Effects Of Light On Growth

Light, in the context of Bonsai, is a dynamic and ever-changing force. It influences not only the rate of growth but also the form, texture, and color of the Bonsai. A tree that basks in the abundance of bright sunlight will narrate a different story than one that grows in the softer, dappled light of a shaded area. The sun-loving tree might boast of compact growth, with smaller leaves and a robust trunk, testament to its journey through the seasons of bright light. In contrast, a tree that thrives in gentler light conditions may develop larger, more delicate leaves, its form a dance of grace and subtlety, a reflection of its more sheltered life.

The direction and quality of light also play pivotal roles in the Bonsai's growth. A tree that receives uneven light may start to lean or grow towards the light source, striving for balance in its quest for light. This natural tendency, known as phototropism, is a dance of survival and adaptation. The bonsai artist, aware of this dance, can manipulate light to influence the tree's shape and direction, guiding it to grow in a desired form.

But light's influence extends beyond growth patterns and physical form; it also touches the very color and texture of the Bonsai. Under the right light conditions, the leaves might develop vibrant hues, rich greens, or even fiery autumnal colors, depending on the species and the season. The bark, too, tells a tale of its interaction with light – a story of textures, shades, and patterns that speak of the tree's age and its journey through time.

In the art of Bonsai, understanding and harnessing the effects of light is akin to understanding the language of the trees. It's about listening to their needs, observing their responses, and creating an environment where light becomes a tool of beauty and expression. As a bonsai artist, your role is to balance the tree's natural tendencies with your artistic vision, using light as your paintbrush to create a living masterpiece.

In essence, the effects of light on bonsai growth are a beautiful synthesis of nature's hand and the artist's touch. It's a testament to the intricate and intimate relationship between a bonsai and its environment, a dance of light and life that unfolds day after day, season after season, in the miniature world of Bonsai.

CHAPTER 5: DETERMINE YOUR CLIMATE, AMOUNT OF SPACE, DEGREE OF LIGHT, AND BREEZE—AND WHICH TREES MAY WORK BETTER IN DIFFERENT CLIMATES?

Understanding your local climate and environment is crucial for selecting the right bonsai species. This subchapter guides you through assessing and matching your conditions with the ideal bonsai for success.

Assessing your environment:

Climate: Identify your USDA Hardiness Zone (in the US) or similar climate classification for other countries. This will determine which trees are viable for your outdoor space.

Space: Consider the space you have available. Outdoor bonsai need protection from extreme elements, while indoor bonsai require sufficient light.

Light: Most bonsai require several hours of direct sunlight daily. Indoor spaces should be bright, with south-facing windows offering the best light conditions.

Breeze: Good air circulation is vital for preventing diseases. However, strong winds can damage trees and dry them out quickly.

Finding your climate zone:

USDA Plant Hardiness Zone Map: planthardiness.ars.usda.gov

This site is invaluable for gardeners in the United States, providing a detailed map to help you determine your specific hardiness zone, which is crucial for selecting plants, including bonsai, that will thrive in your area.

Royal Horticultural Society (RHS) Hardiness Rating: rhs.org.uk

For those in the UK, the RHS offers a hardiness rating system that categorizes plants based on their ability to withstand cold temperatures, helping you choose the right bonsai for your garden.

Australian Bureau of Meteorology: bom.gov.au

This site provides comprehensive climate and weather information for different regions across Australia, aiding in the selection of bonsai species suited to Australian climates.

Environment and Climate Change Canada: weather.gc.ca

Canadians can use this resource to better understand their local climate conditions, including temperature extremes and precipitation patterns, which are important factors in choosing a bonsai.

Selecting Trees for Different Climates:

Temperate Climates (e.g., much of the US and UK): Japanese Maple (Acer palmatum) thrives here, with a stunning display of color in autumn. It is otherwise adaptable and requires protection from the hottest sun and harshest frosts.

Mediterranean Climates (e.g., parts of California, Southern Europe): Olive Tree (Olea europaea) is ideal, tolerating hot, dry summers and cooler, wet winters. It's drought-resistant and thrives in full sun.

Tropical Climates (e.g., Florida, parts of Australia): Ficus species are perfect, with their ability to grow in humid, warm conditions. They're versatile and can be kept indoors if light conditions are met.

Cold Climates (e.g., Canada, Northern Europe): Siberian Elm (Ulmus pumila) can withstand freezing temperatures, making it a robust choice for colder regions. It requires winter protection when temperatures drop significantly.

Considerations

Choosing the right bonsai for your climate not only ensures the health and growth of your bonsai but also reduces maintenance challenges. Always consider the microclimate of your garden or home, as this can significantly affect your bonsai's well-being.

CHAPTER 6: THE FERTILIZING PROCESS FOR BONSAI

Fertilization is a cornerstone of bonsai care, vital for sustaining the miniature trees' health, vigor, and aesthetic appeal. Unlike their wild counterparts, bonsai trees live in limited soil volumes, making them entirely dependent on their caretakers for nutritional needs. This chapter delves into the nuances of fertilizing bonsai, offering insights to ensure your bonsai not only survives but thrives under your care. Understanding the unique requirements of your bonsai, from species-specific needs to seasonal adjustments, is crucial for effective fertilization.

6.1 Understanding Bonsai Fertilizer

Types of Fertilizer: Bonsai fertilizers fall into two main categories: organic and inorganic. Organic fertilizers, derived from natural sources such as fish emulsion, bone meal, or composted manure, release nutrients slowly as they break down, providing a steady nutrient supply. They also improve soil structure and encourage beneficial microbial activity. However, their nutrient levels are generally lower and less precise than inorganic options.

Inorganic fertilizers, manufactured from chemical compounds, offer precise N-P-K ratios and are quickly available to the plant. This can be particularly useful during growth spurts or when addressing specific deficiencies. The downside is the potential for over-fertilization and the lack of soil health benefits provided by organic options.

N-P-K Ratio: The N-P-K ratio on fertilizer packages represents the percentages of nitrogen (N), phosphorus (P), and potassium (K), respectively. Each element serves a different purpose: nitrogen promotes leaf growth, phosphorus supports root development and flowering, and potassium enhances overall health and disease resistance. The ideal N-P-K ratio varies depending on the bonsai's growth stage and species. For example, a higher nitrogen content is beneficial during the growth season, while a balanced or lower-nitrogen fertilizer suits the dormant period.

6.2 Assessing Your Bonsai's Nutritional Needs

Determining the right fertilizer begins with understanding your bonsai's specific needs, which vary by species, age, and health status. Young, vigorously growing bonsai may benefit from higher nitrogen levels to support foliage development, whereas mature, refining trees often require a more balanced approach to maintain their shape and health.

Soil composition also plays a critical role in nutritional needs. Bonsai soil mixes designed for drainage and aeration may require more frequent fertilization than denser soils. Additionally, observing your bonsai's response to fertilization—such as color, growth rate, and leaf size—can provide valuable feedback for adjusting your fertilization regimen.

6.3 Fertilizing Techniques

Application Methods: The method of fertilizer application can significantly impact its effectiveness. Solid fertilizers, either organic or inorganic, are placed on the soil surface and release nutrients slowly over time. This method is favored for its ease of use and gradual nutrient release but requires regular replacement.

Liquid fertilizers are diluted in water and applied during watering, providing immediate nutrient availability. This method allows for precise control over nutrient delivery but requires more frequent application.

Foliar feeding involves spraying diluted fertilizer directly onto the leaves, facilitating quick nutrient uptake. While beneficial for addressing specific deficiencies, it should not replace soil fertilization.

Frequency and Timing: The frequency of fertilization depends largely on the season. During the active growing season (spring and summer), bonsai typically require more frequent fertilization to support growth. In contrast, during the dormant period (late fall and winter), fertilization should be reduced or paused to avoid stimulating untimely growth.

The timing of fertilizer application can also vary with weather conditions, the tree's health, and the specific growth phase. It's crucial to adapt your fertilizing schedule to your bonsai's needs, avoiding a one-size-fits-all approach.

6.4 Over-Fertilizing And Under-Fertilizing:

Understanding the signs of over-fertilizing and under-fertilizing is crucial for maintaining the health of your bonsai. Over-fertilizing can lead to salt buildup in the soil, causing root burn and leaf scorch, while under-fertilizing may result in stunted growth, pale leaves, and a general decline in vigor.

- **Signs of Over-fertilizing:** Yellowing leaves, leaf drop, stunted growth, and a white crust of fertilizer salts on the soil surface are common indicators. To remedy over-fertilization, flush the soil with plenty of water to remove excess salts and temporarily cease fertilization.

- **Signs of Under-fertilizing:** Slow growth, light green or yellow foliage, and a lack of vigor suggest your bonsai may be under-fertilized. Addressing this involves gradually introducing a balanced fertilizer and monitoring the tree's response.

6.5 Special Considerations For Different Bonsai Styles

Each bonsai style, from the majestic Chokkan to the windswept Fukinagashi, may have slightly different fertilization needs based on the tree's form and growth pattern.

- **For vigorous styles like the Chokkan (Formal Upright),** a balanced approach to fertilization supports steady growth and helps maintain the tree's symmetrical shape.

- **In contrast, styles that feature significant deadwood, such as the Sharimiki (Driftwood),** may require less frequent fertilization, as the emphasis is on maintaining rather than promoting growth.

- **For the dense canopies desired in the Yose-ue (Forest Style),** a slightly higher nitrogen content might be beneficial during the growing season to encourage lush foliage.

6.6 Fertilizing Newly Repotted Or Sick Bonsai

Newly repotted or recovering bonsai have unique nutritional needs. After repotting, a bonsai's ability to uptake nutrients is temporarily reduced until new roots develop. Similarly, a sick bonsai may struggle to absorb or utilize nutrients effectively.

- **For Newly Repotted Bonsai:** Wait several weeks before fertilizing to allow the tree to recover and start producing new roots. Begin with a half-strength, balanced fertilizer to avoid overwhelming the tree.

- **For Sick Bonsai:** Identify and address the underlying health issue before adjusting the fertilization regimen. Once the tree begins to recover, a gentle, balanced fertilization can support its return to health. In some cases, supplements like seaweed extract can provide additional support without the risk of over-fertilization.

Conclusion

Fertilizing bonsai is both an art and a science, requiring observation, adaptation, and a deep understanding of your tree's needs. By mastering the fertilizing process, you ensure your bonsai receives the essential nutrients it needs to flourish. Remember, the goal of fertilization is not just growth but the development of a healthy, aesthetically pleasing bonsai that can be enjoyed for generations. As you gain experience, you'll find that your intuition and knowledge guide you to make the best choices for your bonsai family.

CHAPTER 7: OVERWINTERING BONSAI: ENSURING YOUR TREES THRIVE THROUGH WINTER

Overwintering bonsai is a critical aspect of bonsai care, particularly in regions where winter temperatures drop below freezing. This chapter delves into the essential practices to protect your miniature trees during the cold months, ensuring they not only survive but also thrive and return robust in the spring. The process varies significantly between indoor and outdoor bonsai, each requiring specific strategies to address their unique needs and vulnerabilities to cold stress.

Winter poses several risks to bonsai, including frost damage that can harm or kill roots exposed in shallow pots, dehydration from cold winds, and the potential for branches to break under the weight of snow. Understanding how to mitigate these risks is paramount for every bonsai enthusiast.

7.1 Understanding Bonsai Dormancy

Dormancy is a natural, vital process for many plants, including bonsai. It's a period of rest during the colder months when growth slows significantly, and the tree conserves energy to survive winter and prepare for the growth spurt in spring. During dormancy, a tree's metabolic processes slow down, and it requires less water and no fertilization.

Species-Specific Dormancy: Different species of bonsai enter dormancy at varying times and for different durations, influenced by their native habitats. Deciduous trees, for example, will lose their leaves and enter a state of deep dormancy, evident by their bare branches. Evergreens, while remaining green, still undergo a physiological dormancy, reducing their growth and metabolic activities.

Cues for Dormancy: Bonsai trees rely on environmental cues to enter and exit dormancy, primarily temperature and day length. As daylight decreases and temperatures drop in autumn, trees begin to prepare for dormancy, a process that can be disrupted in indoor environments where temperatures and light levels remain constant. It's crucial to mimic or respect these natural cycles for the health of the bonsai.

7.2 Preparing For Winter

Assessing Your Environment: The first step in preparing your bonsai for winter is to understand your local climate, particularly the lowest temperatures your area may experience. The USDA Hardiness Zone map is a valuable tool for this, offering insights into what temperatures to prepare for. Knowing your zone helps determine the specific needs of your bonsai during winter.

Winter Care for Outdoor Bonsai:

Insulating Pots: Protecting the roots from freezing is paramount. Insulation can be achieved by wrapping pots in bubble wrap, burlap, or even burying them in the ground. The goal is to prevent the soil from freezing solid, which can damage or kill the roots.

Sheltering Trees: Providing a physical barrier against wind, snow, and severe cold can be done through cold frames, unheated greenhouses, or placing bonsai under the eaves of a building. The shelter should allow for air circulation while protecting the trees from the harshest elements.

Watering Needs: While bonsai need less water during dormancy, the soil should not be allowed to dry out completely. Water sparingly, ensuring the roots remain slightly moist. The timing and frequency of watering will depend on the sheltering method used and the specific needs of each tree.

Winter Care for Indoor Bonsai:

Indoor bonsai, particularly tropical species, require a stable environment with adequate light, humidity, and warmth through winter. While they do not experience dormancy in the same way as outdoor bonsai, their growth may slow, and care should be adjusted accordingly.

Light: Ensure bonsai receive enough light, which may involve supplementing with grow lights during shorter winter days.

Humidity: Indoor heating can reduce humidity levels significantly. Use humidity trays, misters, or humidifiers to maintain adequate humidity around your bonsai.

Temperature: Keep indoor bonsai away from cold drafts and direct heat sources. A stable, moderate temperature is ideal for most tropical bonsai species.

7.3 Monitoring And Maintenance Through Winter

Regular monitoring throughout the winter months is essential to ensure the well-being of your bonsai. Even in dormancy, bonsai trees are not entirely inactive and can be susceptible to various stresses. Here's how to keep a vigilant eye on them during winter:

Inspect for Pests and Diseases: The cooler months can see an uptick in certain pests and diseases, particularly for indoor bonsai or those in greenhouses. Regularly check the undersides of leaves, branches, and the soil for signs of infestation or illness. Early detection is key to preventing spread and ensuring the health of your bonsai.

Watering During Dormancy: Watering needs significantly decrease during winter, but bonsai should not be allowed to dry out completely. The frequency of watering will depend on several factors, including the species of bonsai, the temperature and humidity of their environment, and the type of sheltering provided. Always check the soil moisture level before watering; it should be slightly dry on top but not throughout the pot. Overwatering can be as detrimental as under-watering, leading to root rot and other issues.

Protection from Extreme Conditions: For outdoor bonsai, sudden drops in temperature or unexpected snowfall can pose risks. Be prepared to provide extra protection on very cold nights, such as moving trees to a more sheltered location or covering them with frost cloth. For indoor bonsai, ensure they are positioned away from cold drafts and heat sources that can dry them out.

7.4 Spring Recovery

As winter fades and signs of spring emerge, your bonsai will begin to exit dormancy and prepare for the active growing season. This transition period is critical and requires careful management to ensure a smooth recovery:

Gradual Reintroduction to Outdoor Conditions: For bonsai that were overwintered indoors or in a protected environment, gradually acclimate them to outdoor conditions. Start by placing them outside in a shaded, sheltered spot for a few hours each day, gradually increasing their exposure to sunlight and the elements over a week or two. This process, known as hardening off, helps prevent shock from sudden changes in temperature and light.

Resuming Regular Care: As your bonsai awaken from dormancy, their water and nutritional needs will increase. Begin watering more frequently, ensuring the soil remains moist but not waterlogged. Resume fertilization with a balanced, slow-release fertilizer to support new growth. However, wait until you see signs of active growth before fertilizing, as premature feeding can stress the tree.

Assessing Winter Damage: Inspect each bonsai for any signs of winter damage, such as broken branches, desiccation, or pest and disease issues that may have arisen. Address these issues promptly through pruning, treatment, or other care adjustments.

Pruning and Styling: Early spring, before the onset of vigorous growth, is an ideal time for major pruning and styling work on many bonsai species. This timing allows the tree to heal quickly and direct energy to new growth.

Transitioning out of winter into the growing season is a delicate phase that sets the stage for the year's growth and development. By attentively managing the spring recovery process, you ensure your bonsai emerge from winter dormancy strong, healthy, and ready to grow.

7.5 Special Considerations

When overwintering bonsai, there are unique scenarios and tree conditions that require special consideration to ensure the health and survival of the trees through the winter months. Addressing these considerations can make a significant difference in the outcome of the overwintering process.

Sensitive and Tropical Species: Tropical and subtropical bonsai species, which are accustomed to warm climates year-round, need to be kept indoors in most temperate climates during the winter. Even within indoor environments, these species may require supplemental lighting and humidity to mimic their natural habitat as closely as possible. It's crucial to avoid placing them near cold drafts or directly next to heat sources, which can create an overly dry environment.

Newly Repotted Bonsai: Bonsai that have been recently repotted are in a vulnerable state and require extra care during their first winter following repotting. The fresh root work and new soil composition can leave them more susceptible to cold damage. For these trees, consider providing additional insulation around the pot and ensuring they are placed in a sheltered location where temperature fluctuations are minimized. Avoid fertilizing newly repotted bonsai until they have shown signs of active growth in the spring.

Bonsai in Training: Young bonsai or those in the early stages of training may not yet have the robust root system or the structural strength to withstand harsh winter conditions without some assistance. For these trees, slightly more protective measures, such as mulching around the base of the tree or using a cold frame, can provide the extra buffer they need to get through the winter safely.

Adjusting Overwintering Strategies by Species: Different bonsai species have varying levels of cold tolerance, and understanding these can help tailor your overwintering strategies to each tree's specific needs. For example, a pine or juniper bonsai may tolerate and even require some degree of cold exposure to enter proper dormancy and cycle through the seasons healthily. In contrast, a maple or azalea may need protection from the coldest temperatures to prevent root damage.

Conclusion

Overwintering bonsai is a nuanced process that requires understanding the unique needs of your bonsai collection and the specific challenges posed by your local climate. By carefully preparing your bonsai for winter, monitoring them throughout the cold months, and attentively managing their recovery in spring, you can help ensure they not only survive but thrive year after year.

The transition from winter to spring is a critical time for bonsai, marking the end of dormancy and the beginning of a new growth cycle. As you gain experience, you'll become more adept at reading the signs your bonsai give, allowing you to adjust care practices dynamically and foster a deep, rewarding connection with these living art forms.

Remember, the goal of overwintering bonsai is not just to protect them from the cold but to ensure they enter the growing season in the best possible condition. With patience, observation, and a bit of preparation, you can master the art of overwintering bonsai, enriching your experience and enjoyment of this fascinating hobby.

CHAPTER 8: PATIENCE AND CARE: GROWING YOUR BONSAI

Welcome to Chapter 8, "Patience and Care: Growing Your Bonsai." This chapter is a journey into the heart of bonsai cultivation, emphasizing the virtues of patience and the importance of consistent care. Bonsai is not just a horticultural practice; it's an art form that requires time, dedication, and a deep understanding of the natural

world. Here, we will explore the long-term development of Bonsai, focusing on how continuous care and attention shape not only the physical appearance of these miniature trees but also their intrinsic health and vitality.

This chapter is designed to guide beginners and experienced enthusiasts through the various stages of a bonsai's life, highlighting the rewards and challenges encountered. We'll delve into the subtleties of managing a bonsai's growth over the years, understanding its changing

needs, and adapting your care techniques as it matures.

Growing a bonsai is a journey that teaches as much about the rhythms of nature as it does about oneself. It's a process that fosters a deep connection between the grower and the tree, a relationship built on mutual respect and understanding. As we progress through this chapter, you'll gain insights into the art of Bonsai that transcend the usual gardening practices, entering a realm where patience, care, and mindfulness are the key ingredients to cultivating not just a tree, but a living work of art.

8.1 Long-Term Development Of The Bonsai

Unlike many other forms of gardening, Bonsai is not about quick results. It's an art form that unfolds slowly, where the growth and changes of the tree are measured not in days or weeks, but often in years. This slow transformation is part of the allure of bonsai cultivation, offering a unique perspective on the natural world and our place within it.

The evolution of form and character

As a bonsai grows, its character and form develop in response to both its natural tendencies and the interventions of the bonsai artist. Early in its life, the focus is on establishing a strong root system and a basic shape. This foundation sets the stage for the tree's future growth and its potential as a bonsai.

Over the years, the Bonsai's appearance will evolve. Branches will thicken, the trunk will develop texture and character, and the foliage will mature, creating a miniature yet ancient-looking tree. Each species of Bonsai has its own rhythm of growth and maturation, and understanding this rhythm is key to guiding the tree through its developmental stages.

Adapting care over time

As a bonsai matures, its care requirements may change. What worked for a young bonsai might not be suitable for an older, more established tree. The Bonsai's watering, feeding, pruning, and repotting need to be adapted as the tree grows.

For instance, an older bonsai may require less frequent but more strategic pruning to maintain its shape and encourage desired growth patterns. Its soil may need to be refreshed less often than a younger tree, but with greater attention to maintaining soil health and structure.

The role of patience and observation

Patience is perhaps the most important virtue in bonsai cultivation. The slow pace of growth in Bonsai teaches patience and offers a meditative respite from the fast-paced modern world. It encourages the practitioner to slow down, observe, and engage with the tree on a deeper level.

Observation is crucial in understanding the needs and responses of the Bonsai. The bonsai artist can make informed decisions about its care by closely observing the tree's growth, leaf color, soil condition, and overall health.

The rewards of long-term cultivation

The rewards of cultivating a bonsai over the long term are manifold. There is a deep sense of satisfaction in nurturing a tree through

its stages of growth, witnessing its transformation, and seeing the impact of your care and efforts. A mature bonsai is not just a beautiful object; it's a living testament to the time, skill, and patience invested in it.

Moreover, the process of growing a bonsai offers a unique connection to nature. It fosters an understanding of the natural cycles of growth and dormancy, the impacts of the changing seasons, and the intricate balance of caring for a living organism. This connection can be deeply grounding and enriching.

In essence, the long-term development of a bonsai is a journey that mirrors life itself – filled with challenges, changes, and growth. It's a journey that requires dedication and patience but offers immense rewards in return. Through this process, bonsai cultivation becomes more than just a hobby; it becomes a lifelong path of learning, discovery, and fulfillment.

8.2 Managing The Bonsai Across Seasons

Caring for a bonsai is a year-round commitment, with each season bringing its own set of tasks and joys.

Spring: a time of awakening

Spring is a period of vigorous growth for most bonsai trees. It's a time when careful attention is needed as the dormant buds burst into life. Pruning, repotting, and beginning the year's fertilization are key activities during this season. It's also a time to gradually reintroduce outdoor Bonsai to more sunlight if they've been protected during winter. Monitoring for pests and diseases is crucial as new growth emerges, as they can be particularly vulnerable during this period.

Summer: vigilance and growth

Summer brings with it the challenge of maintaining the delicate balance of moisture, light, and nutrition. Watering becomes a critical task, especially during hot, dry spells. The Bonsai's rapid growth during these months may require more frequent pruning to maintain shape and encourage denser foliage. This is also the time to enjoy the full beauty of your Bonsai, as it displays its lush, green canopy.

Autumn: preparing for rest

As the days shorten and temperatures drop, bonsai trees begin to prepare for dormancy. This is the time to gradually reduce watering and stop fertilizing, allowing the tree to harden off for winter. Pruning should be minimized during this period to avoid stimulating new growth that the cold could damage. Autumn is a time of spectacular color changes for deciduous trees, offering a visual treat.

Winter: dormancy and protection

Winter is a time of rest for many bonsai species, particularly those from temperate climates. Protection from extreme cold, wind, and frost is essential. While watering is reduced, it's important to ensure that the Bonsai does not completely dry out. Providing sufficient light and humidity for tropical species kept indoors is key during these shorter, darker days.

Through the changing seasons, the bonsai artist's role shifts from that of an active shaper and caretaker to a more passive protector, allowing the tree to follow its natural cycle. This ebb and flow of activity and rest is a response to the tree's needs and a reflection of the natural world's rhythms.

In summary, managing a bonsai across seasons involves a deep understanding of and adaptation to the cyclical nature of plant life. It's about being in tune with the tree's responses to the changing environment and providing the care it needs at each stage of its yearly cycle. This seasonal rhythm of care creates a bond between the bonsai artist and the tree, a connection that deepens with each passing year.

As you guide your Bonsai through the seasons, you'll find that this cyclical journey is not just about the growth and care of the tree but also about personal growth and learning. Each season brings its lessons and rewards, offering a chance to deepen your understanding of and connection to the natural world. The practice of seasonal bonsai care is a beautiful blend of art, science, and mindfulness, a fulfilling journey that enhances both the life of the Bonsai and the life of the bonsai artist.

CHAPTER 9: HEALING AND PROTECTING: MANAGING PESTS AND DISEASES

In Chapter 5, "Healing and Protecting: Managing Pests and Diseases," we turn our focus to an essential aspect of bonsai care that ensures the longevity and health of these miniature trees. Like any other plant, Bonsai are susceptible to various pests and diseases. The confined environment of a bonsai pot and the meticulous care these trees require can sometimes make them more vulnerable to such issues. However, with proper knowledge and timely intervention, most problems can be effectively managed.

This chapter is designed to equip you with the understanding and tools to identify, prevent, and treat common pests and diseases afflicting Bonsai. We'll explore how to recognize the early signs of trouble, which is crucial for quick and effective treatment. You'll learn about the common pests that target Bonsai, from aphids and spider mites to scale insects and mealybugs, and understand the diseases they can spread.

We'll also delve into the various diseases that can affect Bonsai, including fungal infections like root rot and powdery mildew, and how environmental factors like humidity and ventilation play a role in their development. This chapter will guide you through the steps to take when you encounter these issues, including how to choose and apply treatments safely and effectively.

Preventive care is also a key theme of this chapter. We'll discuss strategies to keep your Bonsai healthy and resilient, reducing the likelihood of pest and disease problems. This includes tips on proper watering, feeding, and pruning techniques and advice on maintaining a clean and healthy environment for your Bonsai.

By the end of this chapter, you'll have a comprehensive understanding of how to protect your Bonsai from pests and diseases, ensuring that they continue to thrive and bring beauty to your space.

9.1 Identifying Common Pests

In bonsai care, early identification of pests is crucial for effective management and treatment. This subchapter focuses on familiarizing you with common pests that afflict bonsai trees, their identifying characteristics, and the initial signs of infestation.

Aphids

- **Appearance**: Aphids are small, soft-bodied insects, often green, black, brown, or red. They typically cluster on new growth and the undersides of leaves.
- **Signs**: Look for misshapen, curling, or yellowing leaves. Aphids also excrete a sticky substance known as honeydew, which can attract ants and lead to sooty mold.

Spider mites

- **Appearance**: Spider mites are tiny, spider-like pests, often red or brown. They are hard to see with the naked eye but can be identified by the fine, silky webs they weave on the foliage.

- **Signs**: Indicators include speckled or discolored leaves and, in severe cases, leaf loss. A magnifying glass can help in spotting these minute pests.

Scale insects

- **Appearance**: Scale insects appear as small, brown, or white bumps on the stems and leaves of Bonsai. They are immobile once mature, attaching themselves firmly to the plant.
- **Signs**: Similar to aphids, scales excrete honeydew, leading to sooty mold. Infested areas may also show yellowing or dieback.

Mealybugs

- **Appearance**: Mealybugs are small, soft-bodied insects covered with a white, cottony substance. They are often found in the crevices between branches and leaves
- **Signs**: Look for white, cotton-like clumps on your Bonsai. Like aphids and scale insects, mealybugs produce honeydew, which can lead to sooty mold growth. Infested areas may also exhibit stunted growth or leaf drop.

Whiteflies

- **Appearance**: Whiteflies are tiny, white-winged insects congregating on the undersides of leaves. They fly up in a small cloud when the plant is disturbed.
- **Signs**: Yellowing leaves, stunted growth, and honeydew secretion are common signs of whitefly infestation.

Fungus gnats

- **Appearance**: Fungus gnats are small, dark-colored flies that hover around the soil surface. Their larvae are white or transparent and live in the top layer of the soil.
- **Signs**: Overwatering often leads to fungus gnat problems. The larvae can damage roots, leading to poor plant health.

Preventive measures and initial responses

Regular Inspection: Regularly inspecting your Bonsai is key to early pest detection. Examine the leaves, stems, and soil for any signs of pests.

Isolation: If you detect pests, isolate the affected Bonsai from your other plants to prevent the spread.

Gentle Treatment: Start with gentle treatment options like washing the plant with a strong stream of water or using insecticidal soap. For many pests, early and mild interventions can be effective.

Understanding these common pests and their signs is the first step in protecting your Bonsai. Early detection and appropriate action can prevent minor infestations from becoming serious problems, ensuring the health and beauty of your Bonsai.

Treatment strategies for common pests

Once you've identified a pest infestation, acting swiftly but thoughtfully is important. Here are some effective strategies for treating common pests in Bonsai:

Insecticidal Soap and Horticultural Oils: These are effective against a wide range of pests, including aphids, spider mites, and mealybugs. They work by smothering the pests and are generally safe for the plant when used as directed.

Neem Oil: A natural pesticide, neem oil is effective against various pests and safe for bonsai use. It works as both a repellent and a pest control agent.

Systemic Insecticides: For more severe infestations, systemic insecticides, which are absorbed by the plant and poison pests when they feed on it, can be used. However, they should be used cautiously and as a last resort, as they can be harmful to beneficial insects and the environment.

Physical Removal: In some cases, physically removing pests (like picking off scale insects) can be effective, especially if the infestation is not widespread.

Environmental Controls: Adjusting the environment can help control pests. For example, increasing air circulation and reducing humidity can help control spider mites, which thrive in stagnant, warm conditions.

Regular monitoring and maintenance

After treating for pests, continue to monitor your Bonsai closely for any signs of recurrence. Regular maintenance, including proper watering, feeding, and pruning, can help keep your Bonsai healthy and more resistant to pests.

Preventive measures

Prevention is often the best defense against pests in Bonsai. Here are some key strategies to help prevent infestations:

- **Quarantine New Plants**: Always quarantine new Bonsai or plants before introducing them to your collection to prevent the spread of pests.

- **Maintain Cleanliness**: Keep the area around your Bonsai clean. Remove fallen leaves and debris that can harbor pests.

- **Proper Watering and Fertilization**: Overwatering or under-watering, as well as over-fertilization, can stress your Bonsai, making it more susceptible to pests. Maintain a balanced watering and feeding schedule.

- **Regular Inspection**: Regularly inspect your Bonsai for any signs of pests. Early detection can prevent major infestations.

- **Optimal Growing Conditions**: Ensure your Bonsai is growing in conditions that suit its specific needs. Proper light, temperature, and humidity are crucial for keeping a bonsai healthy and less prone to pest attacks.

- **Use of Beneficial Insects**: Introducing beneficial insects, like ladybugs or predatory mites, can be an effective organic way to control pest populations.
- **Avoid Overcrowding**: Ensure that your Bonsai have enough space for air circulation. Overcrowded plants can create a microclimate that is conducive to pest infestations.

Integrating these preventive measures into your regular bonsai care routine can significantly reduce the likelihood of pest problems. Remember, a healthy bonsai is the best defense against pests and diseases. Consistent care, attention to environmental conditions, and a proactive approach to plant health will go a long way in keeping your Bonsai thriving and pest-free.

9.2 Prevention And Treatment Of Diseases

Bonsai trees, like all plants, are susceptible to a range of diseases. These diseases can be caused by fungi, bacteria, or viruses and often exacerbated by environmental stressors.

Common Bonsai Diseases

Root Rot: Often caused by overwatering, root rot occurs when excess moisture suffocates the roots, leading to decay. Signs include soft, brown roots and a general decline in the tree's health.

Powdery Mildew: This fungal disease appears white, powdery on leaves and stems. It's often caused by poor air circulation and high humidity.

Leaf Spot: Caused by various fungi or bacteria, leaf spot diseases present as discolored spots on leaves, which can lead to leaf drop.

Prevention Strategies

Preventing disease in Bonsai largely revolves around providing optimal growing conditions and practicing good hygiene.

Proper Watering: Avoid overwatering and ensure your Bonsai has well-draining soil to prevent root rot.

Air Circulation and Sunlight: Ensure your Bonsai receives adequate air circulation and sunlight, which can help prevent fungal diseases like powdery mildew.

Cleanliness: Keep the area around your Bonsai clean and free of debris. Disinfect pruning tools between uses to prevent the spread of pathogens.

Regular Inspection: Regularly inspect your Bonsai for early signs of disease. Early detection can make treatment more effective.

Treatment Of Diseases

If your Bonsai does contract a disease, prompt and appropriate treatment is crucial.

Fungicides: Fungicides can be effective for fungal diseases like powdery mildew and leaf spot. Choose a product suitable for the specific disease and follow the application instructions carefully.

Pruning: Remove and destroy affected parts of the plant. For root rot, this may involve pruning away the affected roots and repotting the Bonsai in fresh soil.

Adjusting Care: Often, diseases are a sign of environmental stress. Adjusting your care routine can help address the underlying cause. For example, improving drainage, reducing watering, or increasing light exposure can help combat root rot.

Isolation: If a bonsai is diseased, isolate it from your other plants to prevent the spread of the disease.

Cultural Controls: Sometimes, changing the conditions in which the Bonsai is grown can help control or eliminate the disease. This might include increasing spacing between plants to improve air circulation or adjusting humidity levels.

Chemical Controls: In some cases, especially for severe or persistent diseases, chemical treatments may be necessary. It's important to use chemicals specifically labeled for use on Bonsai or the particular type of plant, and to follow all safety and application guidelines.

Natural and Organic Options: For those who prefer a more natural approach, organic options like neem oil or baking soda solutions can be effective against certain fungal diseases.

Recovery And Aftercare

After treating a bonsai for disease, it's important to continue monitoring the tree closely. Recovery may take time, and the tree may need a period of reduced stress and careful attention to regain its health. This might include providing optimal growing conditions, ensuring proper nutrition, and avoiding major pruning or repotting until the tree has fully recovered.

In conclusion, the prevention and treatment of diseases in Bonsai require a combination of good cultural practices, regular monitoring, and timely intervention. Understanding the common diseases and how to effectively manage them can help ensure your Bonsai remains healthy and vibrant for years to come.

9.3 Long-Term Health Of The Bonsai

Ensuring the long-term health of a bonsai tree is a commitment that involves consistent care, observation, and adaptation to the tree's changing needs.

Regular health checks

Routine Inspection: Regularly inspect your Bonsai for signs of stress, pests, or diseases. This includes examining the leaves, branches, trunk, and roots (during repotting). Early detection of problems is key to effective management.

Leaf and Needle Health: The condition of the leaves or needles provides vital clues to the overall health of the Bonsai. Discoloration, spots, wilting, or abnormal leaf drop can indicate issues ranging from nutritional deficiencies to pest infestations or diseases.

Soil and root care

Soil Quality: Maintaining high-quality soil is crucial for the long-term health of a bonsai. The soil should be well-draining yet retain enough moisture to support the tree's needs. Periodically refreshing or changing the soil can prevent nutrient depletion and soil compaction.

Root Health: Healthy roots are essential for a healthy bonsai. During repotting, inspect the roots for signs of rot or disease. Pruning the roots, when done correctly, can promote a healthy root system and, by extension, a healthy tree.

Nutrition and fertilization

Balanced Feeding: Regular fertilization is important for providing the necessary nutrients. Use a balanced fertilizer suited to your bonsai species and adjust the feeding schedule based on the tree's growth cycle and health.

Monitoring Fertilizer Effects: Observe how your Bonsai responds to fertilization and adjust the type, quantity, and frequency as needed. Over-fertilization can be just as harmful as under-fertilization.

Environmental factors

Light: Ensure your Bonsai receives the appropriate amount of light for its species. Both insufficient light and too much direct sunlight can harm the tree.

Temperature and Humidity: Protect your Bonsai from extreme temperatures and fluctuations. Managing humidity levels, especially for indoor Bonsai, can prevent stress and promote healthy growth.

Pruning and training

Regular Pruning: Regular pruning is not just about maintaining shape; it's also about encouraging healthy growth. Pruning can stimulate new growth and help maintain the tree's vigor.

Gentle Training: While shaping and training are integral to bonsai art, it's important to do so in a way that does not overly stress the tree. Allow periods of rest where the tree can grow without interference.

Stress management

Avoiding Overworking: Continuously stressing a bonsai through excessive pruning, wiring, or repotting can weaken its health. Balance periods of active training with periods of rest and recovery.

Responding to Signs of Stress: If a bonsai shows signs of stress, such as leaf drop or stunted growth, assess your care routine and the environment. It may be necessary to adjust watering, lighting, or feeding practices.

Long-term planning

Anticipating Changes: As bonsai trees age, their care requirements can change. Be prepared to adapt your care strategies to accommodate these changes, such as altered water or nutrient needs, and slower growth rates.

Record Keeping: Keeping a record of your Bonsai's care, including pruning, repotting, and any treatments for pests or diseases, can be invaluable. This history can help you make informed decisions about its future care.

In essence, the long-term health of a bonsai is a result of attentive and adaptive care, a deep understanding of the tree's needs, and a commitment to its ongoing well-being. By nurturing your Bonsai with knowledge, patience, and respect, you can enjoy the rewards of this ancient art form for many years, creating a legacy that can be passed down and appreciated for generations.

CHAPTER 10: THE MAGIC OF PRUNING: SCULPTING YOUR BONSAI

As you embark on the journey of bonsai cultivation, pruning is one of the most transformative skills you will learn. Chapter 3, "The Magic of Pruning: Sculpting Your Bonsai," is dedicated to unraveling the art and science behind this crucial practice. Pruning is not just about maintaining the size of your Bonsai; it's a creative process that shapes the very essence of your tree, influencing its form, structure, and even its health.

In this chapter, we will explore the fundamentals of pruning, from the basic techniques to more advanced strategies for shaping and styling your Bonsai. You'll learn about the different types of pruning, the best times to prune various species, and how to make cuts that encourage healthy growth. We'll also delve into the aesthetic aspects of pruning, helping you understand how to use this technique to express your artistic vision and enhance the natural beauty of your Bonsai.

Whether you are a beginner just starting to shape your first tree or an experienced practitioner looking to refine your skills, this chapter will provide valuable insights and practical guidance to help you master the art of bonsai pruning.

10.1 Fundamentals Of Pruning

Pruning, a central technique in bonsai art, is much more than just cutting away parts of a tree. It is a thoughtful process of decision-making where each cut is made with intention and foresight. This section delves into the essential principles and practices that form the foundation of bonsai pruning.

Understanding growth patterns

To prune effectively, one must first understand how a tree grows. Different species have unique growth patterns, and even individual trees of the same species can vary. Recognizing the direction and vigor of growth, the way a tree heals, and how it responds to cuts is crucial. For instance, some trees may sprout vigorously after pruning, while others might react more conservatively.

Tools for pruning

The right tools not only make the job easier but also ensure clean cuts that heal well. Essential tools for bonsai pruning include:

- **Bonsai Scissors**: Designed for precision, these scissors come in various sizes for different pruning tasks.
- **Concave Cutters**: Used for removing branches, these cutters leave a concave wound that heals with minimal scarring.
- **Knob Cutters**: Similar to concave cutters but with a rounded end, perfect for cutting in tight spaces and creating deep, hollow wounds for better healing.

- **Wire Cutters**: Essential for removing wires used in shaping without damaging the tree.

Techniques of pruning

Pruning techniques vary based on the goal, whether it's shaping the tree, encouraging growth, or maintaining health.

Pinching: This involves removing the tips of new growth to encourage branching and denser foliage. It's commonly used on species like pines and junipers.

Thinning: This technique involves removing entire branches or sections of foliage to improve light penetration and air circulation within the canopy.

Defoliation: Applied to certain deciduous species, defoliation involves removing leaves to reduce leaf size and encourage finer branching.

Timing of pruning

The timing of pruning is as important as the technique itself. Most structural pruning is done during the tree's dormant period, usually in late winter or early spring. This timing allows the tree to heal before the growing season begins. Maintenance pruning, like pinching and thinning, is typically done during the growing season.

Pruning for shape and style

Pruning is also used to shape Bonsai into various styles, such as formal upright, informal upright, cascade, and more. The style chosen often reflects the natural growth habit of the tree but can also be influenced by the artist's vision. Pruning for style involves a careful balance between maintaining the tree's health and achieving the desired aesthetic.

Healing and aftercare

After pruning, proper care is essential to ensure good healing. This includes protecting the tree from extreme conditions, ensuring adequate water and nutrition, and sometimes applying wound sealants to larger cuts.

Developing a pruning strategy

Pruning, in the realm of Bonsai, is an ongoing dialogue between the artist and the tree. It's a process that evolves with the changing seasons and the growing bond and understanding between you and your Bonsai. As you spend more time with your tree, observing its unique growth patterns and responses, you begin to develop a sense of what it needs and how it communicates through its foliage and form.

Imagine pruning as a dance, where sometimes you lead, and at other times, you follow the tree's lead. This dance is not just about the steps (or cuts) you take but about the rhythm and flow of growth that you're trying to harmonize with. When you prune a branch, you're not just shaping the tree; you're redirecting its energy, guiding its growth, and even influencing its future form.

The art of pruning is also about balance and proportion. It's a thoughtful exercise in aesthetics, where each decision to cut or not to cut plays a crucial role in the overall harmony of the tree. This balance isn't just about symmetry; it's about creating a natural, pleasing form that reflects the essence of the tree. It's about enhancing the tree's best features and minimizing any flaws. The goal is to achieve a composition that feels both spontaneous and well-ordered, much like a well-composed piece of music.

Moreover, pruning is about creating depth and perspective. It's akin to sculpting, where you're carving out space, light, and shadow to bring out the tree's character. By selectively thinning out foliage, you can create layers that give the illusion of depth, making the tree appear larger and more majestic than its actual size. This aspect of pruning is particularly fascinating, as it allows a small tree to embody the grandeur of a full-sized tree in nature.

As your Bonsai matures, so does your approach to pruning. What begins as basic shaping evolves into subtle refinements. This evolution in pruning parallels your growth as a bonsai artist. Each cut, each decision, becomes more intuitive and confident as you gain experience. And with each passing season, as you watch your Bonsai respond and flourish, you'll find that pruning becomes more than just a task—it becomes a source of deep satisfaction and personal expression.

10.2 Training And Shaping Techniques

Training and shaping a bonsai is where the true artistry of this ancient practice comes into play. It's a delicate dance between the natural growth of the tree and your vision as an artist. This subchapter delves into the various techniques used to guide and shape a bonsai, transforming it into a living sculpture that embodies both the essence of nature and the bonsai artist's creative expression.

Wiring

Wiring is a fundamental technique in Bonsai used to shape and direct the growth of branches and trunks. It involves wrapping wire around these parts of the tree to gently bend and position them. This technique allows for a high degree of control over the shape of the tree, making it possible to achieve a wide range of styles and forms.

Types of Wire: The two main types of wire used in Bonsai are aluminum and copper. Aluminum wire is softer and easier to bend, making it ideal for beginners and for use on trees with softer wood. Copper wire is stronger and holds its shape better, but it requires more skill to apply without damaging the tree.

Application: When wiring a branch or trunk, the wire is wrapped around in a spiral, ensuring it is close enough to provide support but not so tight as to cut into the bark. The angle of the wire should be around 45 degrees to the branch, providing enough leverage for bending.

Bending: Once wired, the branch can be carefully bent into the desired position. This should be done gradually, over time, to avoid breaking the branch. The flexibility of the branch varies with species, age, and health, so it's important to bend slowly and gently.

Timing: The best time to wire a tree is typically when it is not in active growth, such as in late fall or winter for many species. However, this can vary depending on the tree type.

Monitoring and Removal: Wired branches should be monitored regularly for signs of the wire cutting into the bark, which can cause scarring. The wire is usually removed after one growing season, but this can vary depending on the growth rate of the tree.

Wiring Tips and Techniques

Wiring is a fundamental aspect of bonsai cultivation, allowing you to shape and style your tree according to your vision. However, it's essential to understand the best practices and techniques to ensure successful wiring without causing harm to your tree. Here are some common questions and considerations regarding wiring:

Fitting Mesh Over Drainage Holes: When preparing your bonsai pot for wiring, it's crucial to cover the drainage holes with mesh to prevent soil from escaping. Aim for a mesh size that is small enough to retain the soil but allows for adequate drainage. Typically, a fine mesh with openings no larger than a few millimeters is suitable. You can use various materials for the mesh, including aluminum, ordinary thin garden wire, or copper. Choose a material that is durable and resistant to corrosion, as it will be in constant contact with moisture.

Selecting the Right Wire Size and Type: The size and type of wire you use for wiring your bonsai depend on the tree species, its thickness, and the desired degree of flexibility and strength. Aluminum wire is commonly used for its flexibility and ease of bending, especially for younger and more pliable branches. However, for thicker or more rigid branches, copper wire may be preferred for its superior strength and holding power. When selecting wire size, aim for a diameter that is approximately one-third the thickness of the branch you intend to wire.

Bending Techniques: When bending the wire to create loops or securing it through the drainage holes, consider using a technique that provides stability and prevents damage to the branches or pot. Some bonsai practitioners prefer to bend the wire into "butterfly wing" loops, which distribute the pressure more evenly and reduce the risk of wire cutting into the bark. Additionally, when threading the wire through the drainage holes, ensure that it is bent downward over the straight part with the loops, creating a secure anchor point. Experiment with different bending techniques to find the most effective and secure method for your specific bonsai and pot combination.

Strength and Durability: The strength and durability of the wire are essential factors to consider, especially for long-term styling and training of your bonsai. While both aluminum and copper wire offer sufficient strength for most applications, copper wire is generally stronger and less prone to stretching or breaking under tension. However, keep in mind that copper wire may leave stains on the bark over time, affecting the aesthetic appearance of your bonsai. Evaluate the specific requirements of your tree and choose the wire type that best balances strength, flexibility, and aesthetic considerations.

Application Techniques: There are various techniques for applying wire to bonsai branches, each with its advantages and considerations. Some practitioners prefer to bend the wire into a right-angled "U" shape and then bend it outward after threading it through the drainage holes. Others may opt for the "butterfly wing" technique, with loops positioned strategically to distribute pressure evenly. Experiment with different application methods to find the one that offers the best balance of stability, security, and minimal impact on your bonsai's health.

The timing for wiring your bonsai depends on several factors, including the species of tree, its growth cycle, and the specific styling objectives. In general, the best time to wire bonsai is during the tree's dormant season or periods of reduced growth. For most deciduous trees, this typically occurs in late winter to early spring, before the buds begin to swell but after the threat of freezing temperatures has passed.

Wiring during dormancy allows you to manipulate branches without causing excessive stress or interrupting active growth.

Conversely, for evergreen species such as junipers or pines, the optimal time for wiring is often in late spring or early summer, when the new growth is starting to harden off but is still flexible enough to be shaped. Avoid wiring during periods of active growth, as this can cause damage to the tree and inhibit healthy development.

Pruning

Pruning in Bonsai is used to shape the tree, control its size, and maintain its health. It involves selectively removing parts of the tree, such as branches, leaves, or roots.

Structural Pruning: This is done to shape the basic structure of the Bonsai. It involves removing larger branches and is typically done during the dormant season. Structural pruning is crucial for defining the tree's overall shape and style.

Maintenance Pruning: This type of pruning is performed to maintain and refine the shape of the Bonsai. It involves trimming back new growth to encourage branching and to keep the tree in scale. Maintenance pruning is an ongoing process and is crucial for the tree's aesthetic upkeep.

Root Pruning: During repotting, the roots of the Bonsai are often pruned to encourage the growth of new feeder roots and to ensure the tree remains healthy in its pot. Root pruning is a delicate process that should be done carefully to maintain the health and stability of the tree.

Technique: When pruning, it's important to use sharp, clean tools to make precise cuts. This helps ensure quick healing and reduces the risk of disease. Cuts should be made at an angle to promote water runoff and to blend with the natural shape of the tree.

Healing: After pruning, particularly larger cuts, it's important to care for the wound to promote healing and prevent disease. This may involve applying a wound sealant or paste to protect the exposed wood.

Clipping and pinching

Clipping and pinching are techniques primarily used to refine the foliage and maintain the miniature size of the Bonsai. They are crucial for the aesthetic maintenance of the tree.

Clipping: This involves using scissors to trim back leaves and shoots. Clipping is often used for larger, woodier growth and allows for more precise control over the shape of the foliage. It's a common method for maintaining the desired silhouette of the Bonsai.

Pinching: Pinching is a more delicate technique, usually done with the fingers. It's used to remove the tips of new growth, particularly on conifers like pines and junipers. Pinching helps to encourage denser growth and smaller leaves, which are essential for maintaining the miniature aesthetic of the Bonsai.

Timing and Frequency: Both clipping and pinching are typically done during the growing season. The frequency depends on the growth rate of the tree and the desired level of density and refinement. Fast-growing species may require more frequent trimming.

Selective Removal: When pinching or clipping, it's important to be selective, removing only what is necessary to shape the foliage and encourage desired growth patterns. Over-pruning can weaken the tree and disrupt its natural growth.

Grafting

Grafting in Bonsai adds new elements to a tree, such as branches or roots, or introduces different foliage types.

Types of Grafts: There are several grafting techniques used in Bonsai, including approach grafting, where a branch or seedling is grown close to the trunk and gradually joined to it, and scion grafting, where a piece of a branch (scion) is inserted into a cut in the trunk or a larger branch.

Purpose: Grafting can be used to repair damage, improve the tree's shape, or add new features, such as a branch in a specific location. It's also used to change the leaf type by grafting a different variety onto the existing rootstock.

Process: Grafting requires precise cuts and often the use of grafting tape or sealant to hold the grafted material in place until it heals and integrates with the host tree. The success of grafting depends on factors like compatibility between the scion and rootstock, the timing of the graft, and the environmental conditions.

Aftercare: Post-grafting care is crucial. The grafted area needs to be kept at the right humidity level and protected from extreme temperatures. The tree should not be stressed by other major interventions like repotting or heavy pruning until the graft has fully taken.

Defoliation

Defoliation is a technique used primarily on deciduous bonsai trees to reduce leaf size and increase ramification.

Process: Defoliation involves carefully removing the leaves from a tree, leaving the leaf stems intact. This encourages the tree to produce a new flush of smaller leaves, which are more in proportion with the size of the Bonsai.

Timing: This technique is usually performed in early summer, giving the tree enough time to recover and produce new leaves before the onset of winter.

Selective Defoliation: In some cases, only a portion of the leaves may be removed, known as partial defoliation. This can help balance the vigor of the tree, as removing leaves from a particularly vigorous part of the tree will slow its growth.

Considerations: Defoliation is a stressful process for the tree and should only be performed on healthy, well-established trees. It's also important to provide extra care after defoliation, including protection from strong sunlight and ensuring adequate watering.

Creating deadwood

Creating deadwood, known as Jin (for branches) and Shari (for trunks), involves stripping bark and sapwood to create areas of deadwood, simulating age and exposure to natural elements.

Technique: Tools like jin pliers, knives, and carving tools are used to strip the bark and shape the deadwood. The process should be done carefully to avoid damaging the live parts of the tree.

Aesthetic Purpose: Deadwood features can add a dramatic and aged look to the Bonsai, giving it character and a sense of history. It's particularly common in styles that mimic trees found in harsh, natural environments.

Preservation: After creating deadwood, treating the wood is often necessary to prevent rot and decay. This might involve applying lime sulfur, which also gives the deadwood a bleached, weathered appearance.

Each of these techniques requires a blend of skill, patience, and an understanding of the tree's biology. They are not just methods of shaping but are also ways of communicating with the tree, guiding its growth while respecting its natural tendencies. Mastery of these techniques allows the bonsai artist to create a living work of art, a miniature representation of nature's grandeur.

10.3 Maintenance And Aesthetic Care

In the serene world of Bonsai, the routine of maintenance and aesthetic care transcends the boundaries of mere gardening. It evolves into a deeply personal journey, a meditative practice that connects the bonsai artist with the rhythms of nature. This journey is not just about the physical nurturing of a miniature tree; it's an exploration of patience, attentiveness, and the subtle art of balance.

Imagine those quiet moments with your Bonsai, where time seems to stand still, and the only world that exists is the one within the reach of your fingertips. In these moments, the simple act of watering your Bonsai becomes a reflective practice. It's an opportunity to observe the delicate interplay of light and shadow, feel the texture of the leaves, and witness life's gradual unfolding in a miniature landscape. This daily ritual is more than just a chore; it's a moment of connection, a time to listen to the silent language of your living sculpture.

Pruning and trimming, often perceived as mere horticultural techniques, transform into expressions of creativity in the hands of a bonsai artist. Each decision to cut or not to cut is a brushstroke in an evolving masterpiece. It's a dance of understanding and intuition, where you learn to read the subtle cues of your tree, guiding its growth while honoring its inherent nature. This process is not about dominating the tree but about uncovering its natural beauty and potential, much like an artist revealing the form within a block of marble.

The aesthetic journey of Bonsai also extends to its presentation and the environment it inhabits. The choice of pot, the positioning of the tree, and its relationship with its surroundings are all part of a larger artistic expression. These elements come together to create a harmonious whole, where the Bonsai is not just a plant in a pot but a living piece of art, a reflection of both the natural world and your personal aesthetic.

As the seasons roll from spring's vibrant growth to winter's dormant quiet, your relationship with your Bonsai deepens. Each season brings its own rhythm, its own set of challenges and joys. Adapting to these changes teaches you the art of resilience and flexibility. It's a reminder of the ever-changing nature of life, a lesson in embracing the ebb and flow of existence.

In essence, the ongoing care of a bonsai is a journey that intertwines the art of cultivation with the art of living. It's a practice that nurtures not just the tree but also the soul of the caretaker. Through the rhythms of pruning, watering, and caring, you engage in a dialogue with nature, experiencing a world where every leaf tells a story, and every branch holds a

lesson. This dialogue, this dance with nature, is what makes Bonsai so much more than a hobby or a craft. It's a pathway to mindfulness, a canvas for artistic expression, and a source of deep, enduring satisfaction.

As you tend to your Bonsai, you're not just shaping a tree; you're engaging in a form of active meditation. Each action, whether it's adjusting a wire or trimming a leaf, is done with intention and focus. This mindful engagement brings a sense of tranquility and presence, offering a respite from the hustle and bustle of everyday life. The Bonsai becomes a sanctuary, a space where calm and peace are cultivated alongside the tree.

Moreover, the aesthetic care of your Bonsai is a reflection of your journey as an artist and a caretaker. Over time, as you learn and grow, your approach to bonsai care evolves. What begins as a tentative exploration becomes a confident expression of your unique vision. Your Bonsai becomes a testament to your dedication, a living embodiment of your growth and learning.

In the end, the maintenance and aesthetic care of Bonsai are about forming a bond with a piece of the natural world. It's a relationship that grows stronger and more profound with each passing season, a partnership that teaches and enriches in equal measure. Through the art of Bonsai, you embark on a journey of discovery, where the rewards extend far beyond the physical beauty of the tree. It's a journey that nurtures the soul, enriches the mind, and brings beauty to life.

CHAPTER 11: STYLES AND FORMS: ARTISTIC EXPRESSION IN BONSAI

Chapter 10, "Styles and Forms: Artistic Expression in Bonsai," invites you into the diverse and captivating world of bonsai styles. This chapter isn't just a catalog of different forms; it's an exploration of how each style reflects a unique blend of cultural history, artistic interpretation, and deep understanding of the natural world.

Bonsai, as an art form, offers a rich tapestry of styles, each with its own story and aesthetic appeal. From the formal upright's stately elegance to the cascade's dramatic poise, these styles are more than just templates; they are expressions of the natural environment and the artistic vision of the bonsai creator.

In this chapter, we delve into the essence of various traditional bonsai styles, exploring their origins, characteristics, and the techniques used to achieve them. We'll look at how each style seeks to replicate certain aspects of nature, whether it's the windswept trees on a cliff edge or the majestic poise of a forest giant.

But the art of bonsai is not static. It's a living, evolving form of expression. Thus, we also explore how modern interpretations and personal creativity play a significant role in contemporary bonsai. This chapter celebrates the innovation and individuality that modern bonsai artists bring to these traditional forms.

Through this exploration, you'll gain insights into not just how these styles are created, but why they are cherished. You'll learn how the choice of tree species, the shaping techniques, and even the selection of the pot and stand contribute to the overall aesthetic and narrative of the bonsai.

Whether you are a seasoned bonsai enthusiast or a curious beginner, this chapter will deepen your appreciation for the artistry behind bonsai cultivation. It's a journey through the myriad ways a simple tree, in the hands of a skilled artist, can become a living masterpiece, a testament to the beauty and complexity of nature and human creativity.

11.1 Overview Of Bonsai Styles

In the world of bonsai, style is not just a form but a narrative. Each style tells a story, evoking images of the natural landscapes from which these miniature trees draw their inspiration.

Each bonsai style offers a window into the natural world and the artist's interpretation of it. Understanding these styles is not just about learning techniques; it's about appreciating the stories they tell and the emotions they evoke. As we further explore these styles, we'll delve into the nuances that make each unique and the skills required to achieve them.

As an art form, Bonsai is rich in diversity and creativity, with each style representing a unique aspect of nature and artistic interpretation. Let's explore and expand upon the various bonsai styles, each with its distinct characteristics and aesthetic appeal.

Formal upright (chokkan)

The Chokkan style is one of the most classic and elegant bonsai forms, embodying the essence of tranquility and strength. It is characterized by its simplicity and symmetry, reflecting the natural growth of trees in open, undisturbed environments. Here are the defining characteristics of the Chokkan style:

- **Trunk:** The trunk is straight and upright, tapering gradually from the base to the apex. This tapering gives the illusion of depth and distance, making the tree appear larger and more majestic.
- **Branches:** Branches are arranged symmetrically and in a balanced manner around the trunk, with the lowest branches being the longest and upper branches progressively shorter. This arrangement contributes to the pyramid-like silhouette of the tree.
- **Apex:** The apex is directly above the base of the trunk, continuing the vertical line without leaning to any side. It is usually formed by the extension of the trunk itself rather than by an upper branch.
- **Roots:** The root base (nebari) is evenly spread around the trunk, providing a stable and visually appealing foundation that enhances the tree's upright posture.

Practical Steps to Create a Bonsai in the Chokkan Style

Creating a Chokkan bonsai involves careful selection and meticulous shaping to achieve its distinguished upright form. Here's a step-by-step guide:

1. Selection of Material:

- Opt for a tree with a naturally straight trunk or one that can be trained upright. Species with a strong central leader and even growth are ideal.
- Ensure the tree has a well-developed nebari and potential for symmetric branch development.

2. Initial Styling:

- **Wiring:** If necessary, apply wire to the trunk early in the development to correct any slight deviations from vertical. Wiring can also be used on branches to position them more horizontally.
- **Shaping:** The goal is minimal in terms of bending; focus on ensuring the trunk grows perfectly upright.

3. Branch Selection and Pruning:

- Identify and select branches to create a balanced, symmetrical silhouette. The first branch should be approximately one-third of the way up the trunk, extending horizontally.
- Prune to encourage a clear hierarchical structure, with each successive branch up the trunk shorter than the one below it.

4. Potting and Positioning:

- Choose a pot that complements the formal style; often, a simple, unglazed, rectangular or oval pot works well.

- Center the tree in the pot to emphasize its symmetry and formality. The tree should be planted so that it stands upright, reinforcing the vertical line from the base to the apex.

5. Maintenance and Refinement:

- Regular pruning is essential to maintain the clear structure of the branches and the overall shape of the tree. This includes removing any growth that disturbs the symmetry.
- Monitor and adjust the tree's position and straightness as it grows, especially after repotting.

6. Periodic Re-evaluation:

- As the bonsai matures, continue to assess and refine its shape. This may involve selective pruning to enhance the taper of the trunk or thinning the canopy to ensure the symmetrical distribution of foliage.

Informal upright (moyogi)

The Moyogi style, or Informal Upright, is one of the most popular and versatile styles in bonsai cultivation. It mimics the natural growth patterns of trees in their native environments, offering a balance between the strict formality of the Chokkan (Formal Upright) and the more dramatic shapes seen in other styles. Here are its defining characteristics:

- **Trunk:** The trunk of a Moyogi bonsai exhibits gentle curves or movements, yet the apex of the tree aligns vertically with the base, maintaining an overall upright form. The trunk's movement adds visual interest and a sense of dynamism.

- **Branches:** Branches are typically arranged in a balanced manner, with the first branch emerging from the lower third of the trunk, extending to one side. Subsequent branches alternate sides as they ascend, contributing to the tree's overall balance and natural appearance.

- **Apex:** The apex is well-developed and continues the line established by the trunk, reinforcing the tree's upright stance despite the trunk's curves.

- **Roots:** The root base (nebari) is visibly spread and stable, anchoring the tree visually and physically. A well-developed nebari enhances the tree's appearance of age and stability.

Practical Steps to Create a Bonsai in the Moyogi Style

Creating a Moyogi bonsai involves several stages, from selecting the right material to ongoing care and styling. Here's how to start:

1. Selection of Material:

- Choose a tree with a naturally curved or slightly slanted trunk. Species with flexible trunks and branches are ideal, as they can be further shaped through wiring and pruning.

- Look for a tree with a good branch structure that can be developed into the alternating pattern characteristic of the Moyogi style.

2. Initial Styling:

- **Wiring:** Apply wire to the trunk and main branches to guide their growth and shape. The wiring should be done carefully to avoid damaging the bark, using wire that's approximately one-third the thickness of the branch or trunk.

- **Shaping:** Gently bend the trunk and branches to enhance their natural curves. The goal is to create movement in the trunk while ensuring the apex remains aligned with the base.

3. Branch Selection and Pruning:

- Identify the primary branches, starting with the lowest one, which should extend from the trunk at about one-third the tree's height. Remove any branches that disrupt the tree's balance or clutter its silhouette.

- Prune back overly long branches to encourage ramification and create a dense, leafy canopy.

4. Potting and Positioning:

- Choose a pot that complements the tree's size and style. The pot should be understated, allowing the tree to be the focal point.
- When potting, position the tree slightly off-center in the pot for visual balance, considering the direction of the trunk's movement.

5. Maintenance and Refinement:

- Continue to prune and wire the tree as it grows, maintaining the desired shape and encouraging the development of secondary and tertiary branches.
- Regularly monitor the tree's health, adjusting watering, feeding, and light exposure to support its growth.

6. Periodic Re-evaluation:

- As the bonsai matures, periodically re-evaluate its shape and structure. This may involve adjusting the wiring, pruning to refine the shape, or even changing the potting angle to enhance the tree's appearance.

Broom (hokidachi)

The Hokidachi style, or Broom Style, is celebrated for its natural, harmonious appearance, closely resembling the shape of a full, leafy broom. This style is particularly suited to deciduous trees with fine branching patterns that can create a dense, rounded canopy atop a straight trunk. Here are the defining characteristics of the Hokidachi style:

- **Trunk:** The trunk is straight and upright, extending from the base to about one-third of the tree's total height, where it abruptly divides into many fine branches.
- **Branches:** The branches radiate outward in all directions from the point where the trunk ends, creating a symmetrical, dome-shaped canopy. The branches and twigs are evenly distributed, contributing to the full, rounded appearance of the canopy.
- **Apex:** The apex is not defined by a single branch but is instead formed by the collective tip of the canopy, contributing to the broom's rounded silhouette.
- **Roots:** The root base (nebari) should be well-developed and evenly spread around the trunk, providing a stable and aesthetically pleasing foundation that supports the upright growth.

Practical Steps to Create a Bonsai in the Hokidachi Style

Creating a Hokidachi bonsai involves careful branch selection and meticulous canopy shaping to achieve its distinctive broom-like appearance. Follow these steps to cultivate your Broom Style bonsai:

1. Selection of Material:

- Choose a deciduous species with a naturally straight trunk and the potential for dense branching. Species like Zelkova, Japanese Maple, or certain types of Elm are ideal.
- Look for a specimen with a clear, unblemished trunk that can be trained into the upright form necessary for the Hokidachi style.

2. Initial Styling:

- **Wiring:** Minimal wiring may be needed, primarily to correct any slight curves in the lower trunk to ensure it remains straight.
- **Branch Selection:** Early on, identify and select branches at the trunk's division point that can be developed into the symmetrical canopy. Remove any branches below this point to emphasize the clear trunk.

3. Developing the Canopy:

- **Pruning:** Regular pruning is required to encourage a dense branching structure. Trim back longer branches to promote back-budding and the development of fine twigs.
- **Canopy Shaping:** Shape the canopy by pruning to maintain a rounded, dome-like silhouette. This will likely involve more frequent pruning during the growing season to keep the shape compact and balanced.

4. Potting and Positioning:

- Choose a shallow, wide pot that complements the broad canopy of the Hokidachi style. The pot should not overshadow the tree but rather support its visual impact.
- Center the tree in the pot to highlight its symmetry. The straight trunk should be prominently displayed, leading up to the expansive canopy.

5. Maintenance and Refinement:

- Continue to refine the canopy's shape through selective pruning, always aiming to maintain the broom's characteristic rounded form.
- Pay attention to the health of the tree, ensuring it receives adequate light, water, and nutrients to support the dense foliage of the canopy.

6. Periodic Re-evaluation:

- As the tree matures, periodically assess the overall shape and density of the canopy. It may be necessary to thin the interior branches to allow light and air to penetrate, ensuring the health of the tree and maintaining the desired form.

Slanting (shakan)

The Shakan style, or Slanting style, captures the essence of trees that grow in nature under challenging conditions, such as strong winds or heavy snows, causing them to lean in one direction. This style is marked by its dynamic movement and the impression of resilience and adaptation. Here are the defining characteristics of the Shakan style:

- **Trunk:** The trunk leans at an angle from the base, creating a sense of movement and direction. Despite the slant, the trunk should exhibit a smooth, natural flow without abrupt bends.
- **Branches:** Branches typically grow more vigorously on the side opposite the lean, as if reaching for sunlight. The arrangement is asymmetrical, balancing the visual weight of the slanted trunk.
- **Apex:** The apex of the tree leans in the same direction as the trunk, reinforcing the impression of wind or weight influencing the tree's growth.
- **Roots:** The root base (nebari) on the side opposite the lean is often more developed, visually anchoring the tree and supporting its slanted posture.

Practical Steps to Create a Bonsai in the Shakan Style

Creating a Shakan bonsai involves careful planning and styling to convincingly portray a tree shaped by natural forces. Follow these steps to cultivate your Slanting Style bonsai:

1. Selection of Material:

- Choose a tree with a naturally inclined trunk or one that can be trained to slant. Species with flexible trunks are preferable, as they can be gently guided into the desired angle.
- Ensure the tree has potential for asymmetric branch development, which is crucial for achieving balance in the Shakan style.

2. Initial Styling:

- **Wiring:** Apply wire to the trunk and main branches to guide their growth in the slanted direction. The wiring should be done thoughtfully to encourage a natural curve that enhances the tree's dynamic posture.
- **Angle Adjustment:** Gradually adjust the tree's angle by repotting it in the desired slant or using guy wires to pull the trunk towards the intended lean.

3. Branch Selection and Pruning:

- Prioritize the development of branches that will counterbalance the slant of the trunk. This often means selecting stronger, more vigorous branches on the side opposite the lean.
- Prune to encourage a harmonious distribution of foliage, ensuring the tree remains visually balanced despite its slant.

4. Potting and Positioning:

- Choose a pot that complements the slanted form. Oval or rectangular pots can provide a stable base and enhance the visual flow of the slanting trunk.
- Position the tree off-center in the pot, with the lean directed slightly towards the viewer, to increase the sense of depth and movement.

5. Maintenance and Refinement:

- Continue shaping the tree through pruning and wiring, always mindful of enhancing the slanted form and maintaining visual balance.
- Regularly adjust the tree's position and the tension of guy wires if used, to ensure the slant develops as intended without compromising the tree's health.

6. Periodic Re-evaluation:

- As the bonsai matures, reassess its form and structure. The slant may need to be accentuated or moderated based on the tree's growth and the development of its branches and roots.

Windswept (fukinagashi)

The Fukinagashi style, or Windswept style, embodies the force of nature, specifically the strong, unidirectional wind that shapes trees in their natural habitat. This style is dramatic and evocative, capturing the struggle and resilience of trees against the elements. Here are the defining characteristics of the Fukinagashi style:

- **Trunk:** The trunk may start upright but then bends significantly to one side, as if being blown by the wind. The degree of the bend can vary, but it consistently leans in one direction, illustrating the force of the wind.
- **Branches:** Branches and foliage are swept to one side, mimicking the effect of continuous wind. Branches on the windward side (facing the direction of the wind) are often sparse or entirely absent, while the leeward side (opposite the wind) shows denser foliage.
- **Apex:** The apex of the tree follows the direction of the trunk and branches, leaning strongly to one side, enhancing the windswept illusion.
- **Roots:** The root base (nebari) on the windward side may be more exposed, suggesting soil erosion due to the wind, whereas the leeward side might show roots more securely anchored in the soil.

Practical Steps to Create a Bonsai in the Fukinagashi Style

Creating a Fukinagashi bonsai requires an artistic vision to convincingly portray the effects of wind on a tree. Here's how to cultivate your Windswept Style bonsai:

1. Selection of Material:

- Opt for a tree with a flexible trunk that can be trained into the windswept form. Species that naturally grow in windy areas or have flexible branches are ideal.
- The initial shape of the tree doesn't need to be perfect; the styling will create the windswept effect.

2. Initial Styling:

- **Wiring:** Carefully apply wire to the trunk and branches to guide them into the windswept shape. The wiring should be strategic, aiming to create a coherent flow that suggests movement by the wind.
- **Shaping:** Bend the trunk and branches to one side, creating a uniform direction in the tree's form. The degree of bending should reflect the strength of the wind you wish to depict.

3. Branch Selection and Pruning:

- Emphasize the development of branches on the leeward side of the tree, pruning to encourage growth that complements the windswept direction.
- Remove or minimize branches on the windward side to enhance the effect of the wind sweeping across the tree.

4. Potting and Positioning:

- A shallow, elongated pot can accentuate the horizontal spread of the branches and foliage. The choice of pot should harmonize with the dramatic movement of the tree.
- Position the tree in the pot so that the direction of the perceived wind is clear and the composition is balanced, with the tree's form extending dynamically across the pot.

5. Maintenance and Refinement:

- Continue to guide the tree's growth through selective pruning and wiring, maintaining the windswept illusion as the tree matures.
- Adjustments may be needed over time to reinforce the directionality and to manage the density of the foliage on the leeward side.

6. Periodic Re-evaluation:

- As your bonsai develops, regularly assess its form and the effectiveness of the windswept illusion. The style may evolve as the tree grows, requiring creative adjustments to preserve the narrative of resilience against the wind.

Twin trunk (sokan)

The Sokan style, or Twin Trunk style, is a fascinating bonsai form that features two trunks emerging from a single root system. This style symbolizes harmony and balance, often representing a parent and child or two partners standing together. The visual appeal of Sokan lies in the interaction between the two trunks and how they complement each other in size, shape, and foliage. Here are the defining characteristics of the Sokan style:

- **Trunks:** One trunk is typically larger and taller, considered the "parent," while the other is smaller and slightly shorter, representing the "child." Both trunks grow from the same root base, with their forms and lines harmonizing with each other.

- **Branches:** The branching on each trunk should reflect the overall style and balance of the tree. The larger trunk will usually have more extensive branching, while the smaller trunk's branching is more modest, ensuring that the focus remains balanced between the two.

- **Apex:** Each trunk has its own apex, with the parent trunk's apex being higher and more developed. The apices should complement each other, contributing to the tree's overall harmony.

- **Roots:** The root base (nebari) is shared and should be well-developed and balanced, providing a stable and aesthetically pleasing foundation for the two trunks.

Practical Steps to Create a Bonsai in the Sokan Style

Creating a Sokan bonsai involves careful planning and execution to ensure that the two trunks coexist in harmony and enhance each other's beauty. Here's how to cultivate your Twin Trunk Style bonsai:

1. Selection of Material:

- Choose a tree species that naturally produces multiple trunks or can be encouraged to do so through techniques like air layering or grafting. Species with flexible growth habits and the ability to back bud on old wood are ideal.

- Look for material where the two trunks naturally emerge close to the ground and exhibit potential for harmonious development.

2. Initial Styling:

- **Wiring:** Apply wire to both trunks if necessary, guiding their growth in a way that emphasizes their relationship. The larger trunk should grow upright or slightly slanted, while the smaller trunk may lean away or follow a complementary curve.

- **Shaping:** Shape the trunks so that they appear as natural extensions of each other, with the smaller trunk subtly echoing the form of the larger one.

3. Branch Selection and Pruning:

- Develop the branches on each trunk with the overall composition in mind. The goal is to create a canopy that unifies the two trunks while respecting their individuality.

- Prune to maintain the visual dominance of the larger trunk, ensuring that the smaller trunk complements rather than competes with it.

4. Potting and Positioning:

- Select a pot that accommodates the spread of the two trunks and their root system. A slightly larger pot may be necessary to provide balance and stability.
- Position the tree in the pot to highlight the interaction between the two trunks, with the larger trunk often placed slightly off-center for visual balance.

5. Maintenance and Refinement:

- Continue to refine the shape and relationship between the two trunks through selective pruning and wiring. Pay special attention to the development of the canopy, ensuring it enhances the twin trunk form.
- Regularly assess the health and growth of both trunks, adjusting care practices to support their harmonious development.

6. Periodic Re-evaluation:

- As the bonsai matures, reassess the dynamic between the two trunks. Changes in growth or form may necessitate adjustments to maintain the aesthetic and symbolic balance of the Sokan style.

Clump (kabudachi)

The Kabudachi style, also known as the Clump Style, is a distinctive bonsai form that features multiple trunks emerging from a single root system. This style mimics a natural occurrence where several trees grow together as a clump, often seen in forests where trees sprout from a single seed cluster or rootstock. The Kabudachi style is celebrated for its complex beauty and the sense of a miniaturized, dense forest it conveys. Here are the defining characteristics of the Kabudachi style:

- **Trunks:** Several trunks of varying thicknesses and heights emerge from the same point at the base, creating a dynamic and intricate visual effect. The trunks should have a natural, organic arrangement, with each contributing to the overall composition.

- **Branches:** The branches on each trunk extend outward and upward, contributing to a shared canopy that unites the individual trunks into a cohesive whole. The branching pattern should ensure that each trunk is visible and plays a part in the overall structure.

- **Apex:** Each trunk may have its own apex, but together, they form a unified canopy. The variation in apex heights adds depth and realism to the clump, enhancing its forest-like appearance.

- **Roots:** The shared root base (nebari) is a critical feature, providing stability and aesthetic appeal. A well-developed nebari reinforces the impression of age and natural growth.

Practical Steps to Create a Bonsai in the Kabudachi Style

Creating a Kabudachi bonsai involves nurturing a group of trunks to grow in harmony, presenting a unique challenge in balance and design. Here's how to cultivate your Clump Style bonsai:

1. Selection of Material:

- Opt for species that naturally produce suckers or multiple trunks from the base. Species that can be propagated from cuttings planted closely together are also suitable.

- Initial material should ideally show a natural tendency to form a clump, with several trunks already emerging from or near the base.

2. Initial Styling:

- **Wiring:** Individual trunks may be wired to enhance their shape or direct their growth, but the wiring should respect the natural form of the clump. Avoid over-manipulating, which might detract from the organic feel.

- **Shaping:** Arrange the trunks to ensure that each has its space and contributes to the overall silhouette. The arrangement should look natural, as though the trunks grew together spontaneously.

3. Branch Selection and Pruning:

- Develop the branches to create a dense, shared canopy. Prune to maintain the individuality of each trunk while ensuring they come together to form a harmonious whole.

- Regular pruning is necessary to manage the growth of the trunks and maintain the forest-like appearance of the clump.

4. Potting and Positioning:

- A wider, shallow pot is often suitable for the Kabudachi style, providing space for the spread of the trunks and roots. The pot should complement the natural, untamed look of the clump.
- Position the clump in the pot to allow each trunk room to express its character while maintaining the collective impact of the group.

5. Maintenance and Refinement:

- Continue to refine the shape of the trunks and the canopy, ensuring that the clump remains balanced and visually appealing. The goal is to foster a sense of unity among the trunks while preserving their individual strengths.
- Pay attention to the health of the entire clump, ensuring that all trunks receive adequate light, water, and nutrients.

6. Periodic Re-evaluation:

- As the bonsai matures, reassess the arrangement and growth of the trunks. Adjustments in pruning and positioning may be needed to enhance the clump's overall beauty and maintain its forest-like essence.

Forest (Yose-ue)

The Yose-ue style, or Forest Style, is a mesmerizing bonsai form that simulates a miniature forest or grove of trees growing together. This style is profound in its ability to convey the essence of a natural landscape within a confined space, offering a multi-dimensional viewing experience. The Yose-ue style is characterized by its grouping of multiple trees of the same species, varying in size and height to mimic depth and perspective. Here are the defining characteristics of the Yose-ue style:

- **Trunks:** The composition includes multiple trunks of varying thicknesses and heights, typically an odd number, arranged to create a natural-looking woodland scene. The tallest tree, often placed off-center, acts as the main focal point.

- **Branches:** Branches are pruned and arranged to ensure that each tree contributes to the overall canopy, with careful attention to avoid overcrowding. The arrangement allows for open spaces and layers, enhancing the forest effect.

- **Apex:** Each tree within the group has its own apex, contributing to the collective canopy. The variation in apex heights across the trees adds to the perception of depth and realism in the miniature forest.

- **Roots:** Trees share a common container, with their roots intertwined below the soil. The arrangement at the base should provide stability and contribute to the natural, cohesive appearance of the forest setting.

Practical Steps to Create a Bonsai in the Yose-ue Style

Creating a Yose-ue bonsai requires an artistic vision and strategic planning to replicate the complexity and beauty of a natural forest. Here's how to cultivate your Forest Style bonsai:

1. Selection of Material:

- Choose young trees of the same species with varying trunk diameters and heights. Using trees of the same species ensures uniform growth conditions and aesthetic coherence.

- Seedlings or young plants that can be grouped closely are ideal. Consider the natural growth habits and canopy shapes of your chosen species to enhance the forest effect.

2. Initial Styling:

- **Grouping:** Arrange the trees in the container starting with the tallest tree slightly off-center. Surround it with progressively smaller trees, placing them to create depth and perspective. The arrangement should look organic, as if the trees naturally grew together.

- **Wiring and Shaping:** Minimal wiring may be applied to individual trees to adjust their angles or direct growth. The aim is to complement the forest composition without making any single tree appear overly manipulated.

3. Branch Selection and Pruning:

- Prune branches to prevent overcrowding and to ensure that each tree has its space within the canopy. The goal is to mimic the way trees in a forest compete for light, leading to upward growth and open spaces between them.
- Regular pruning helps maintain the forest's layered look, with taller trees having higher canopies and smaller trees filling in the lower layers.

4. Potting and Positioning:

- A shallow, wide tray or pot is typically used to accommodate the group planting and to emphasize the landscape effect. The choice of container should reflect the natural setting you wish to emulate.
- Ensure the trees are planted firmly, with their roots spread out to establish a stable base for the forest.

5. Maintenance and Refinement:

- Continue to refine the arrangement as the trees grow, trimming branches and adjusting placements as necessary to maintain the forest's balance and proportion.
- Monitor the health of all trees, providing consistent care to support the collective growth of the forest.

6. Periodic Re-evaluation:

- As the bonsai forest matures, periodically reassess its overall appearance. Changes in the growth pattern of individual trees may require adjustments to preserve the intended landscape effect.

Raft (Ikada-buki)

The Ikadabuki style, or Raft Style, is a captivating bonsai form that simulates the natural occurrence of a tree fallen over in nature, with new vertical growth sprouting along the horizontal trunk. This style is remarkable for its storytelling ability, depicting resilience and renewal. Trees in the Ikadabuki style are characterized by their lateral trunk lying almost parallel to the soil, with branches growing upward as if they were individual trees. Here are the defining characteristics of the Ikadabuki style:

- **Trunk:** The main trunk lies horizontally on the soil surface or slightly buried, simulating a tree that has fallen over. The trunk may show natural curves, enhancing the visual flow of the composition.

- **Branches:** Branches emerging from the horizontal trunk grow vertically, mimicking the appearance of a row of trees or a natural forest. These branches are trained to become the new 'trunks', varying in height to create depth and interest.

- **Apex:** There is no single apex in the traditional sense. Instead, each vertical branch acts as an individual apex, contributing to the collective canopy of the raft.

- **Roots:** The original root system of the horizontal trunk remains important, but new roots often develop at the base of the vertical branches, securing them into the soil and enhancing the illusion that each branch is a separate tree.

Practical Steps to Create a Bonsai in the Ikadabuki Style

Creating an Ikadabuki bonsai involves simulating the natural process of a tree adapting to environmental changes. This style requires patience and vision to achieve the desired effect. Here's how to cultivate your Raft Style bonsai:

1. Selection of Material:

- Choose a tree species that naturally produces multiple shoots from the trunk and is flexible enough to be laid horizontally. Species with a strong ability to back bud along the trunk are ideal.

- The tree should have a relatively long trunk and a healthy branch structure capable of simulating individual trees.

2. Initial Styling:

- **Laying the Trunk:** Carefully lay the trunk horizontally on the soil surface, securing it in place. Portions of the trunk can be slightly buried to encourage root growth from the underside.

- **Wiring and Shaping Branches:** Apply wire to the branches that will serve as the new vertical 'trunks'. Gently guide their growth upward, ensuring a natural, varied appearance among them.

3. Branch Selection and Pruning:

- Select branches along the horizontal trunk to develop as the new vertical growth. These should be spaced to mimic natural tree spacing in a forest.

- Prune the branches to encourage upward growth and to maintain the overall health and balance of the composition. The goal is to create a canopy that reflects a group of trees growing in close proximity.

4. Potting and Positioning:

- A long, shallow pot is typically used for the Ikadabuki style to accommodate the horizontal trunk and allow space for the vertical branches to develop. The pot should complement the naturalistic setting you're aiming to recreate.
- Position the horizontal trunk within the pot, considering how the vertical branches will fill the space as they mature.

5. Maintenance and Refinement:

- Continue to guide the growth of the vertical branches, trimming them to maintain their individual tree-like appearances. This includes managing the development of their canopies and ensuring a harmonious overall composition.
- Encourage root growth from the underside of the horizontal trunk to enhance stability and the illusion of a natural raft formation.

6. Periodic Re-evaluation:

- As the bonsai matures, reassess the arrangement and growth of the vertical branches. Adjustments may be necessary to preserve the narrative of a fallen tree giving life to a new forest.

Cascade (kengai)

The Kengai style, or Cascade style, is one of the most dramatic and visually striking bonsai forms. It emulates trees that grow on steep cliffs or in mountainous regions, where they might hang downward due to gravitational forces, snow loads, or other environmental factors. The Cascade style is characterized by a trunk that grows upward from the soil line only to dramatically cascade downward, often extending below the base of the pot. Here are the defining characteristics of the Kengai style:

- **Trunk:** The trunk initially grows upward for a short distance, then bends sharply downward, extending below the pot's rim. The trunk may continue to curve and twist, adding to the dramatic effect.

- **Branches:** Branches grow outward from the cascading trunk, arranged to balance the composition and add fullness to the tree's silhouette. The branches are pruned and positioned to mimic the natural growth patterns of trees under extreme conditions.

- **Apex:** In the Cascade style, the apex is located at the lowest point of the tree, contrary to more traditional styles where the apex is at the top. This inverted apex reinforces the downward growth habit and the illusion of hanging off a cliff.

- **Roots:** The roots must be strong and well-established in the pot to support the cascading trunk and branches. A solid root base is crucial for stability and health.

Practical Steps to Create a Bonsai in the Kengai Style

Creating a Kengai bonsai requires careful planning and execution to achieve the desired dramatic effect while ensuring the tree's health and stability. Here's how to cultivate your Cascade Style bonsai:

1. Selection of Material:

- Choose a species that naturally adapts to cascading or can be trained to grow downward. Species with flexible trunks and a good response to wiring are ideal.

- The initial material should have a trunk that can be shaped into the cascade form and branches that can be developed along the cascading line.

2. Initial Styling:

- **Wiring:** Apply wire to the trunk and main branches to guide them into the cascading form. The wiring should be done carefully to encourage the desired shape without damaging the tree.

- **Shaping:** Bend the trunk downward, ensuring a smooth transition from the upward growth to the downward cascade. The trunk should extend below the pot's rim, with the branches arranged to complement this dramatic form.

3. Branch Selection and Pruning:

- Develop branches along the cascading trunk, pruning to create a balanced silhouette. The branches should be positioned to add depth and interest, with the foliage distributed evenly to enhance the tree's aesthetic appeal.

- Regular pruning is necessary to maintain the shape and health of the cascade, encouraging compact growth and the development of fine branching.

4. Potting and Positioning:

- A deep pot or one specifically designed for cascade bonsai is used to accommodate the downward growth. The pot should be sturdy enough to counterbalance the weight of the cascading trunk and branches.
- Position the tree in the pot so that the cascading trunk is securely anchored, with the roots well-established to support the tree's dramatic form.

5. Maintenance and Refinement:

- Continue to refine the cascade shape through selective pruning and wiring. Adjustments may be needed as the tree grows to enhance the cascade effect and maintain the overall composition.
- Ensure the tree receives adequate care, including watering, feeding, and protection from extreme weather, to support its health and development.

6. Periodic Re-evaluation:

- As the bonsai matures, periodically reassess its form and structure. The cascade style may evolve, requiring creative adjustments to preserve its dramatic impact and visual harmony.

Semi-cascade (han-kengai)

The Han-Kengai style, or Semi-Cascade style, represents a less extreme version of the Cascade style, where the tree's trunk extends over the edge of the pot but does not drop as significantly below the pot's rim. This style simulates the natural growth of trees on mountain ledges or over water, where gravity influences their growth to a certain extent, but they do not hang as dramatically as in the full Cascade style. Here are the defining characteristics of the Han-Kengai style:

- **Trunk:** The trunk grows upright from the soil for a short distance before curving downward, extending over the pot's edge but not far below it, creating a graceful, semi-cascading effect.
- **Branches:** Branches emerge from the trunk, arranged to balance the composition and add visual interest. They are pruned and positioned to enhance the semi-cascade form, contributing to the overall aesthetic of the tree.
- **Apex:** The apex in the Semi-Cascade style is typically located just above or at the rim of the pot, reinforcing the impression of a tree growing in a challenging environment but with a somewhat upright resilience.
- **Roots:** A strong, well-established root system is crucial for anchoring the tree in the pot, providing the necessary support for the semi-cascading trunk and branches.

Practical Steps to Create a Bonsai in the Han-Kengai Style

Creating a Han-Kengai bonsai involves a delicate balance between portraying the influence of gravity and maintaining a sense of uplift. Here's how to cultivate your Semi-Cascade Style bonsai:

1. Selection of Material:

- Opt for species that are flexible and can be trained into the semi-cascade form. Look for a tree with a trunk that naturally leans or can be wired to achieve the semi-cascading shape.
- Consider the natural growth habits of the species to ensure it can adapt well to the semi-cascade style.

2. Initial Styling:

- **Wiring:** Apply wire to the trunk and branches to guide their growth into the desired semi-cascade shape. The wiring should be strategic, aiming to create a natural curve that suggests a gentle downward growth influenced by environmental factors.
- **Shaping:** Bend the trunk so that it extends over the edge of the pot, curving downward without dropping too far below the pot's rim. Arrange the branches to complement this form, ensuring they contribute to the semi-cascade effect.

3. Branch Selection and Pruning:

- Select branches that reinforce the semi-cascade structure, pruning to encourage a balanced distribution of foliage. The branches should be positioned to create depth and to fill out the composition, making the tree appear lush and well-proportioned.

- Regular pruning helps maintain the shape of the semi-cascade, promoting healthy growth and the development of fine branching.

4. Potting and Positioning:

- A deeper pot may be used for the Han-Kengai style compared to the full Cascade style, providing stability and aesthetic harmony with the semi-cascading trunk.
- Position the tree in the pot to highlight the curve of the trunk and the semi-cascade form. The tree should be securely anchored, with the roots spread evenly to support the composition.

5. Maintenance and Refinement:

- Continue refining the semi-cascade shape through selective pruning and wiring. Adjustments may be needed as the tree grows to enhance the semi-cascade effect and maintain visual balance.
- Care for the tree with consistent watering, feeding, and protection from adverse conditions to ensure its health and vitality.

6. Periodic Re-evaluation:

- As the bonsai matures, reassess its form and structure. The semi-cascade style may evolve, requiring creative adjustments to preserve its elegance and balance.

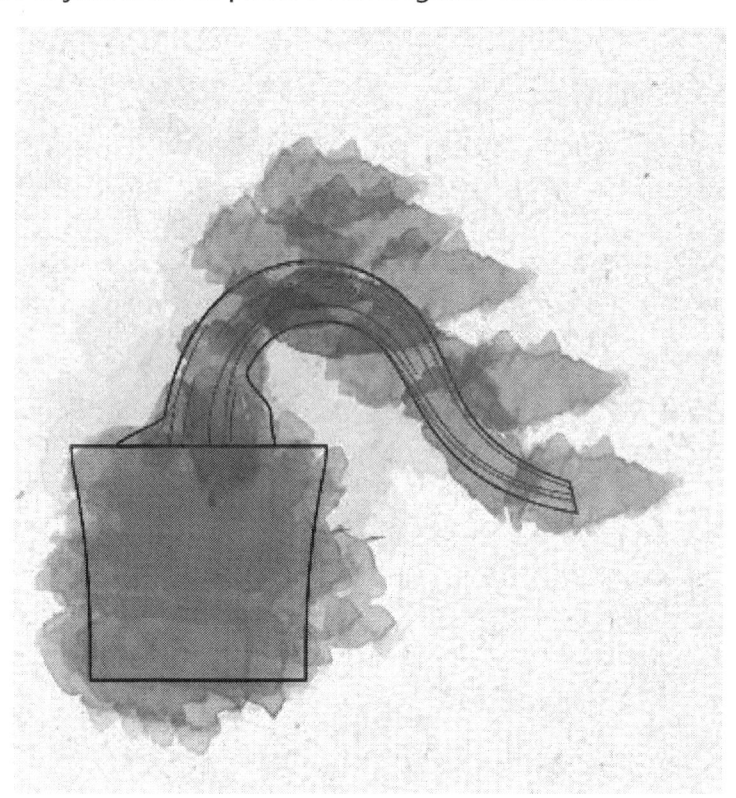

In rock (ishitsuki)

The Ishitsuki style, or Rock Clinging style, is a unique and visually striking bonsai form that simulates trees growing in rocky crevices or on cliffs where roots wrap around rocks to reach the soil. This style emphasizes the symbiotic relationship between the tree and the stone, with the rock often serving as both a visual and structural element of the composition. Here are the defining characteristics of the Ishitsuki style:

- **Trunk and Roots:** The tree's trunk grows up and around a rock, with roots visibly clinging to and wrapping around the stone. The roots may penetrate into crevices in the rock, suggesting a struggle for survival and adaptation to the harsh growing conditions.

- **Branches:** Branches extend outward from the trunk, balanced in a way that complements the form of the rock and the direction of the tree's growth. The branches are pruned to highlight the relationship between the tree and the rock, enhancing the natural beauty of the composition.

- **Rock:** The rock is a central element of the Ishitsuki style, chosen for its shape, texture, and character. It should be aesthetically pleasing and proportionate to the tree, contributing to the overall impression of age and endurance.

- **Placement:** The placement of the tree and rock together is carefully considered to create a harmonious and natural-looking composition. The best arrangements suggest a long-standing bond between the tree and the rock, with the tree adapting to the contours of the stone.

Practical Steps to Create a Bonsai in the Ishitsuki Style

Creating an Ishitsuki bonsai requires an artistic eye for selecting and matching the tree to the right rock, as well as patience and skill in cultivating their relationship. Here's how to cultivate your Rock Clinging Style bonsai:

1. Selection of Material:

- Choose a tree species that naturally exhibits strong root growth and can adapt to growing in confined spaces, such as pines, junipers, or maples.

- Select a rock with an interesting shape and texture that complements the tree you have chosen. The rock should have crevices or holes that can accommodate the tree's roots.

2. Initial Styling:

- **Attaching the Tree to the Rock:** Secure the tree to the rock using safe, non-damaging methods, such as soft ties or wires, ensuring that the roots make contact with the rock's surface. Over time, the roots should grow to cling naturally to the rock.

- **Root Work:** Gently encourage the tree's roots to enter the crevices of the rock, if possible, or to wrap around the rock's form. This may involve careful placement and securing of the roots during potting.

3. Branch Selection and Pruning:

- Prune the branches to create a balanced, aesthetically pleasing shape that enhances the visual impact of the tree-rock composition. The goal is to direct attention to the interaction between the tree and the rock, showcasing their interdependence.

4. Potting and Positioning:

- Pot the tree and rock together in a container that is large enough to accommodate the rock's base and allows for proper drainage. The container should be visually understated to keep the focus on the tree and rock.
- Position the composition in the pot to ensure stability and to best display the relationship between the tree and the rock. The arrangement should look as natural as possible, as if discovered in the wild.

5. Maintenance and Refinement:

- Continue to care for the tree, paying special attention to watering, as the rock may affect the soil's moisture retention. Fertilize appropriately to support the tree's health and growth.
- As the tree matures, periodically adjust the pruning and styling to maintain the desired shape and to reinforce the tree's connection to the rock.

6. Periodic Re-evaluation:

- Over time, reassess the tree and rock composition, making adjustments as needed to accommodate the tree's growth and to enhance the natural beauty of the arrangement.

Literati (bunjin)

The Bunjin style, also known as the Literati style, is inspired by the ancient Chinese literati paintings that depict trees growing in harsh, remote locations with elegant and exaggerated forms. This bonsai style is celebrated for its artistic expression and minimalistic approach, focusing on the line and movement of the trunk with sparse foliage. Here are the defining characteristics of the Bunjin style:

- **Trunk:** The trunk is typically slender and may exhibit dramatic curves or twists, embodying a sense of struggle or adaptation to challenging environments. The trunk's movement is the focal point, often conveying a sense of grace and resilience.
- **Branches:** Branches are few and placed strategically, usually higher up on the trunk, to emphasize the tree's form and movement. The foliage is minimal, not overwhelming the trunk's elegance.
- **Apex:** The apex is often slender and extends in line with the trunk's overall movement, reinforcing the tree's expressive form.
- **Roots:** The root base (nebari) is usually understated, supporting the trunk's slender form without drawing attention away from the line and movement of the tree.

Practical Steps to Create a Bonsai in the Bunjin Style

Creating a Bunjin bonsai is an exercise in artistic restraint and appreciation for the natural beauty of trees. This style allows for personal expression within the framework of bonsai art. Here's how to cultivate your Literati Style bonsai:

1. Selection of Material:

- Choose a species with a naturally flexible trunk that can be shaped into the Bunjin style's characteristic curves. Pine, juniper, and certain deciduous species are often used for their ability to embody the style's aesthetic.
- Look for material with a trunk that already shows some natural movement or character that can be enhanced through styling.

2. Initial Styling:

- **Wiring:** Apply wire to the trunk and any branches to gently guide them into the desired shape. The wiring should be subtle, aiming to enhance the natural curves or create new ones that express the tree's unique story.
- **Shaping:** Focus on creating a trunk line that is visually interesting and conveys a sense of elegance. The branches should be minimal, so the trunk's form becomes the centerpiece of the composition.

3. Branch Selection and Pruning:

- Keep branches to a minimum, selecting a few that can be positioned to complement the trunk's line. Prune back any excess growth to maintain the style's characteristic sparse foliage.
- The branches and foliage should appear almost as an afterthought, with the emphasis remaining on the trunk's movement and form.

4. Potting and Positioning:

- A small, understated pot is ideal for the Bunjin style, as it should not compete with the tree's artistic form. The pot serves more as a base than a feature of the composition.
- Position the tree in the pot to enhance its form and movement. The tree may be placed off-center to increase the visual impact of its curves.

5. Maintenance and Refinement:

- Continue to refine the tree's shape through careful pruning and wiring as it grows. The aim is to preserve the elegance and simplicity of the Bunjin form, allowing the tree's natural beauty to shine.
- Ensure the tree receives appropriate care, focusing on the basics of watering, feeding, and light to keep it healthy while maintaining its minimalistic style.

6. Periodic Re-evaluation:

- As the bonsai matures, periodically reassess its form and structure. The Bunjin style is dynamic, and the tree's expression may evolve. Adjustments may be necessary to maintain or enhance the tree's literati character.

Driftwood (sharimiki)

The Sharimiki style, also known as the Driftwood style, is a dramatic and visually compelling bonsai form that features live veins of foliage alongside areas of deadwood, creating a stark contrast that symbolizes endurance and survival. This style is particularly evocative, representing the tree's struggle against harsh environmental conditions. Here are the defining characteristics of the Sharimiki style:

- **Deadwood:** The most striking feature of the Sharimiki style is the presence of significant deadwood areas on the trunk and sometimes branches. This deadwood, which can be naturally occurring or artificially created, is often bleached and treated to preserve its appearance and contrast with the living parts of the tree.

- **Live Veins:** Narrow strips of live bark run along the trunk and branches, connecting the foliage to the roots. These live veins are crucial for the tree's survival, as they transport nutrients and water between the roots and leaves.

- **Foliage:** The foliage in the Sharimiki style is typically sparse, emphasizing the tree's struggle and resilience. The placement of foliage is strategic, highlighting the live veins and creating visual balance with the deadwood.

- **Trunk and Branches:** The trunk may twist or contort, adding to the dramatic effect. Branches, when present, are often styled to complement the movement and texture of the deadwood and live veins.

Practical Steps to Create a Bonsai in the Sharimiki Style

Creating a Sharimiki bonsai involves careful planning and execution to balance the elements of deadwood and live growth. Here's how to cultivate your Driftwood Style bonsai:

1. Selection of Material:

- Choose a species that responds well to the creation of deadwood, such as juniper, pine, or certain deciduous trees. The tree should have a strong, healthy section of live bark and the potential for creating or enhancing deadwood features.

- Look for material with natural character or the potential to develop an interesting deadwood feature through carving or stripping.

2. Creating Deadwood:

- **Deadwood Creation:** Carefully remove the bark and cambium layer in selected areas to create deadwood features. Techniques such as carving, stripping, or jinning (creating deadwood branches) can be used to enhance the tree's character.

- **Preservation:** Treat the deadwood with lime sulfur or similar products to preserve the wood and give it a bleached appearance, contrasting beautifully with the live parts of the tree.

3. Styling Live Veins and Foliage:

- Carefully preserve and enhance the live veins that connect the foliage to the roots. These should be clearly defined against the deadwood.

- Prune and style the foliage to complement the dramatic deadwood features, ensuring the tree remains balanced and aesthetically pleasing.

4. Potting and Positioning:

- Select a pot that complements the dramatic nature of the Sharimiki style. The pot should not detract from the tree's striking features but rather support the overall composition.
- Position the tree in the pot to showcase the best view of the deadwood and live veins, considering the balance and movement of the composition.

5. Maintenance and Refinement:

- Continue to refine the deadwood and live veins as the tree matures. Additional carving or treatment may be necessary to maintain the desired effect.
- Regularly care for the tree, focusing on the health of the live veins and foliage. Proper watering, feeding, and light are crucial for the tree's vitality.

6. Periodic Re-evaluation:

- As the bonsai develops, periodically reassess the balance between the deadwood and live growth. The Sharimiki style is dynamic, with the potential for ongoing refinement and adjustment to enhance its dramatic impact.

Each bonsai style offers a unique window into the natural world and the bonsai artist's interpretation of it. These styles are not just about shaping trees; they are about capturing the essence of nature's diversity and resilience, each telling its own story of survival, beauty, and adaptation.

11.2 Creating Specific Styles

Creating specific bonsai styles is an art that combines botanical knowledge with artistic vision

Understanding the Tree's Natural Inclinations

The first step in creating a specific bonsai style is to understand the natural growth tendencies of your tree. Each species has its unique characteristics and growth habits, which can lend themselves to certain styles more naturally than others. For instance, a tree with a naturally curved trunk may be well-suited for an Informal Upright or Slanting style.

The Role of Pruning in Shaping

Pruning is a critical tool in defining and maintaining the style of a bonsai. Through selective pruning, you can encourage growth in desired areas, shape the tree's overall structure, and create the aesthetic balance characteristic of the chosen style. Pruning is not just about removing unwanted growth; it's about envisioning the future shape of the bonsai and making strategic cuts to guide it towards that vision.

Wiring and Training

Wiring is another essential technique used to shape bonsai trees. By carefully wrapping wire around branches and trunks, you can gently guide them into the desired position. This is particularly important in styles like the Cascade or Windswept, where branches need to be trained to grow in unconventional directions. The key is to apply the wire thoughtfully, considering both the tree's health and the intended style.

Incorporating Aesthetics and Balance

Creating a specific bonsai style is also an exercise in aesthetics. It involves a deep understanding of balance, proportion, and visual harmony. The placement of branches, the angle of the trunk, and the distribution of foliage all contribute to the overall beauty of the bonsai. In styles like the Forest or the Clump, the challenge is to create a cohesive composition that balances multiple elements.

Adapting and Experimenting

While traditional styles provide a framework, bonsai is also about adaptation and experimentation. Feel free to experiment with blending elements from different styles or creating your variations. The goal is to create a bonsai that not only

reflects a specific style but also resonates with your personal artistic expression. This creative freedom is what makes bonsai a continually evolving art form.

Patience and Persistence

Remember, creating a specific bonsai style is a process that unfolds over time. It requires patience, persistence, and a willingness to learn from both successes and setbacks. The tree will grow and respond at its own pace, and part of the artistry is adapting to its changing needs and growth patterns.

Reflecting on the Artistic Journey

As you work on shaping your bonsai, it becomes a reflection of your journey as an artist. Each decision, from the initial choice of style to the ongoing care and shaping, is a step in a larger artistic process. The bonsai becomes a living canvas, where your skills and vision come to life.

In conclusion, creating specific bonsai styles is a blend of art, science, and intuition. It's about harmonizing the natural tendencies of the tree with the principles of bonsai styling and your unique creative touch. Each bonsai becomes a unique work of art, a testament to the time and care invested in it. This journey of shaping and styling is not just about the end result, but about the relationship that develops between the bonsai artist and the tree. It's a dialogue, where each response of the tree guides the artist's next step.

Embracing the Evolution

As your bonsai matures, its style may evolve. Branches grow, trunks thicken, and the tree's character deepens. Embracing this evolution is part of the bonsai journey. What starts as a Slanting style may gradually take on characteristics of a Windswept form, or a young tree styled as a Formal Upright may develop nuances that lean towards an Informal Upright as it ages. This natural progression adds depth and history to your bonsai, making it a living story of adaptation and growth.

The Joy of Sharing

Finally, sharing your bonsai and its style with others can be a source of joy and inspiration. Whether it's through participating in bonsai clubs, exhibitions, or

simply displaying your bonsai in your home, each bonsai becomes a conversation piece, a shared experience of beauty and nature. It's an opportunity to connect with others who appreciate the art and to inspire those who are new to it.

In the world of bonsai, each style is more than a set of rules; it's a living expression of nature's diversity and the human touch. As you cultivate and style your bonsai, you become part of a centuries-old tradition, a community of artists who find joy and meaning in shaping these miniature reflections of the natural world.

In essence, the journey of creating specific bonsai styles is as enriching as it is challenging. It's a path of continuous learning, where each tree can become a lifelong companion, a source of beauty, and a testament to the art of bonsai.

11.3 Creativity And Personal Expression In Bonsai

In the realm of bonsai, the convergence of creativity and personal expression with traditional practices gives this art form its unique and enduring appeal.

Bonsai, at its core, is an art form – a canvas where nature and nurture blend under the artist's guiding hand. While traditional styles provide a foundation, the true essence of bonsai lies in how each artist interprets and adapts these guidelines to reflect their personal aesthetic and the story they wish to tell. This creative process is deeply personal, often influenced by an individual's journey, connection with nature, and artistic influences.

The act of choosing a tree, shaping it, and even selecting the pot and display, are all decisions steeped in personal expression. For some, bonsai is a reflection of their own life experiences, with each tree representing a particular aspect of their journey or a connection to a memory or emotion. For others, it's an exploration of artistic themes, drawing inspiration from various forms of art, be it painting, sculpture, or even music, and translating these influences into the living medium of bonsai.

Incorporating creativity into bonsai does not mean disregarding the traditional rules but rather understanding and respecting these guidelines while exploring how they can be adapted. It's about finding a balance between honoring the past and embracing the present, between respecting the tree's natural form and guiding it to express something new and personal.

This creative freedom allows for the evolution of bonsai, ensuring that it remains a dynamic and growing art form. Modern bonsai artists continue to push the boundaries, experimenting with new species, unconventional styles, and innovative display methods. These explorations contribute to the individual artist's growth and the broader bonsai community, inspiring others and fostering a culture of continuous learning and experimentation.

The beauty of personal expression in bonsai is that there is no right or wrong way to approach it. Each bonsai artist brings their unique perspective, leading to a diverse and rich tapestry of styles and forms. Whether it's a minimalist approach focusing on the subtle nuances of shape and texture or a more dramatic interpretation playing with bold forms and contrasts, each bonsai becomes a unique piece of art, a testament to the artist's creativity and vision.

In summary, creativity and personal expression are what breathe life into bonsai, transforming it from a mere horticultural practice into an art form. It's a journey of discovery, where each artist explores their relationship with nature and expresses it through the miniature world of bonsai. Through this process, bonsai becomes a reflection of the natural world and a mirror of the self, a canvas for personal storytelling and artistic expression.

CHAPTER 12: REPOTTING: RENEWING YOUR BONSAI'S ROOTS

Welcome to Chapter 6, "Repotting: Renewing Your Bonsai's Roots," where we delve into an essential aspect of bonsai care that rejuvenates and sustains the tree's health. Repotting is more than just a maintenance task; it's a vital process that ensures the longevity of your Bonsai by refreshing the soil, managing root growth, and maintaining the tree's overall health.

This chapter will explore the when, why, and how of repotting Bonsai. Understanding the timing of repotting is crucial, as it varies depending on the species, the age of the tree, and its growth rate. We'll discuss how to recognize the signs that indicate it's time to repot and the steps to do it effectively without causing undue stress to your Bonsai.

Repotting involves carefully removing the tree from its pot, pruning the roots, and replacing the old soil with fresh, nutrient-rich soil. This chapter will guide you through each of these steps, providing detailed instructions and tips to ensure a successful repotting. We'll also cover the selection of the appropriate soil and pots, which play a significant role in the health and growth of your Bonsai.

Repotting can sometimes be intimidating, especially for beginners, but it is a critical component of bonsai care. It not only addresses the immediate needs of the tree, such as root crowding and soil exhaustion but also provides an opportunity to inspect the root system for any signs of disease or decay. Properly executed, repotting invigorates the Bonsai, promoting healthier growth and a more robust life.

Additionally, this chapter will touch upon the aesthetic aspects of repotting. Choosing the right pot that complements your Bonsai's style and size can significantly enhance its overall appearance. The pot is an integral part of the Bonsai's presentation, and its selection is as much an art as it is a practical necessity.

By the end of this chapter, you will have a comprehensive understanding of the repotting process and be equipped with the knowledge and confidence to undertake this crucial task. Repotting is not just about maintaining your Bonsai; it's about actively participating in its growth and evolution, ensuring that it continues to thrive and bring beauty to your life.

12.1 When And How To Repot

Embarking on the journey of repotting a bonsai is to engage intimately with the very foundation of its life – the roots. In the world of Bonsai, repotting is a ritual that goes beyond mere maintenance; it's a renewal, a rebirth of sorts, that ensures the continued health and aesthetic grace of these living sculptures. This subchapter is not just about the mechanics of repotting but about understanding its rhythm and role in the life cycle of your Bonsai.

The art of repotting begins with an understanding of timing, an aspect that is less about adhering to a calendar and more about reading the signs and needs of your tree. Each species of Bonsai, with its unique growth pattern and rate, tells its own story of when it's time to repot. Some trees, vigorous and fast-growing, may beckon for repotting every couple of years, while others, more sedate in their growth, can thrive longer before needing this rejuvenation. The signs are there in the roots that begin to circle the pot or in the soil that seems exhausted, no longer retaining water as it once did.

But repotting is more than just a response to these physical cues; it's a dance with the natural cycle of the tree. For many Bonsai, the ideal time to repot is in the early spring, just as the buds begin to swell, signaling a new cycle of growth. This timing allows the tree to recover and establish itself in its new environment during the growing season. However, this timing can vary based on the tree's species and the local climate, requiring the bonsai artist to be both observant and adaptable.

As you prepare to repot, it's not just about choosing the right soil or the new pot – though these are important elements. It's about approaching the process with a sense of reverence and care. Gently freeing the tree from its old pot, carefully pruning its roots, and placing it in its new home – these steps are performed with a mindfulness that respects the tree's delicate balance. The fresh soil you add is not just a medium but a new foundation, rich with the promise of nutrients and life.

In repotting, there is also an opportunity for aesthetic contemplation and decision-making. The choice of the new pot – its size, shape, color, and texture – is a crucial aspect of the Bonsai's presentation. This choice reflects not just the tree's needs but also your vision for its future growth and character. The pot is a frame that enhances the tree's beauty, a partner in its presentation.

Through the process of repotting, you engage deeply with your Bonsai, gaining a greater understanding of its needs and nuances. It's a process that strengthens the bond between the artist and the tree, a moment of connection that is as rewarding as it is essential. In the end, repotting is a vital step in the journey of bonsai cultivation, a step that ensures your tree continues to grow, thrive, and inspire.

12.2 Selecting Soil And Pots

The selection of soil and pots for Bonsai is an artful endeavor, deeply intertwined with the health and aesthetic of these miniature trees

The art of choosing soil

Selecting the right soil for Bonsai is about understanding the delicate balance of aeration, water retention, and nutrient availability. The ideal soil mix does not follow a one-size-fits-all formula; it varies depending on the species of the Bonsai, the climate, and even the specific conditions in which the Bonsai is kept.

Components of Bonsai Soil: Typically, bonsai soil is a blend of various components, each serving a specific purpose. Akadama, a type of Japanese clay, is often used for its ability to retain water and nutrients while still providing good drainage. Pumice and lava rock contribute to aeration and drainage, preventing soil compaction. Organic components like pine bark can also be included to add structure and retain moisture.

Customizing the Mix: The key is to customize the soil mix to suit the specific needs of your Bonsai. For instance, a moisture-loving tropical bonsai may require more organic material in its soil mix, whereas a desert species like a juniper may thrive in a grittier, more inorganic mix.

Selecting the right pot

Choosing a pot for your Bonsai is much more than just picking a container; it's an integral part of the Bonsai's overall composition and aesthetic.

Size and Proportion: The pot should be proportionate to the size of the Bonsai. A general rule of thumb is that the pot's length should be approximately two-thirds the height of the tree. However, this can vary based on the style and shape of the Bonsai.

Style and Color: The style and color of the pot should complement the Bonsai. For example, a pot with straight lines and a subdued color might suit a formal upright bonsai, while a cascading bonsai might be paired with a deeper, more ornate pot.

Drainage and Functionality: Beyond aesthetics, the pot must be functional. Good drainage is essential to prevent waterlogging and root rot. The pot should also have adequate wiring holes to secure the Bonsai in place.

The harmony of soil and pot

The combination of the right soil and pot is a harmonious marriage supporting the Bonsai's health and beauty. The soil provides the foundation for growth, offering the right mix of nutrients, water, and air. The pot, on the other hand, is the stage on which the Bonsai presents itself to the world, an extension of its identity and character.

In Bonsai, every element is a thoughtful decision, a part of the story that each tree tells. The soil and pot are not mere components; they are essential characters in this narrative, playing a crucial role in the life and art of Bonsai.

CHAPTER 13: THE BONSAIST'S WORKSHOP: ESSENTIAL TOOLS AND MATERIALS

Welcome to Chapter 9, "The Bonsaist's Workshop: Essential Tools and Materials." This chapter is dedicated to the tools and materials that form the backbone of bonsai cultivation. Just as a painter needs brushes and a sculptor needs chisels, a bonsai artist requires specific tools to shape, care for, and nurture these miniature trees.

In this chapter, we will explore the variety of tools and materials that are essential in the art of bonsai. From the basic to the more specialized, each tool has its specific purpose and function in the creation and maintenance of a bonsai. Understanding these tools, how they are used, and how to care for them will enhance your bonsai practice, making the process more efficient and enjoyable.

We'll also delve into the supplementary materials that are often used in bonsai cultivation. These include various types of soil, fertilizers, and pots, each contributing to the health and aesthetic of the bonsai. Selecting the right materials is crucial for the well-being of your trees and can significantly impact their growth and development.

Whether you are setting up your first bonsai workshop or looking to expand your existing toolkit, this chapter will provide you with the knowledge and insights needed to make informed choices about the tools and materials you use in your bonsai journey. By the end of this chapter, you'll have a comprehensive understanding of what you need to create and maintain beautiful bonsai.

13.1 Overview Of Necessary Tools

In the realm of bonsai, having the right tools is essential for the precision and care required to cultivate these miniature trees. Each tool in a bonsaist's workshop serves a specific purpose, helping to shape, prune, and care for the bonsai in a way that respects its delicate balance.

Pruning tools

Pruning is a fundamental aspect of bonsai shaping and maintenance, and having the right pruning tools is crucial. These include:

- **Bonsai Scissors**: Designed specifically for bonsai, these scissors are sharp and precise, ideal for trimming leaves and small branches. Their design allows for clean cuts that heal quickly, minimizing stress on the plant.

- **Concave Branch Cutters**: These are used for removing larger branches. The concave design allows for cuts that heal with minimal scarring, maintaining the aesthetic integrity of the bonsai.

- **Knob Cutters**: Similar to concave cutters but with a rounded end, knob cutters are used for creating hollows or removing small knobs, helping to create a more natural appearance.

Wiring tools

Wiring is another key technique in shaping bonsai, and it requires tools that can handle wire efficiently without damaging the tree.

- **Wire Cutters**: Essential for cutting the bonsai wire, these cutters allow for precise control and help prevent damage to the tree when removing wire.
- **Pliers**: Useful for bending and twisting wire when shaping branches, pliers help in applying wire neatly and effectively.

Soil and repotting tools

Repotting is a critical part of bonsai care, and having the right tools for handling soil and roots can make a significant difference.

- **Root Rakes and Hooks**: These tools are used to gently remove soil from around the roots during repotting, allowing for careful inspection and pruning of the root system.
- **Soil Scoops**: Useful for adding and removing soil from the pot, soil scoops come in various sizes to accommodate different pot sizes.

Miscellaneous tools

- **Brushes**: Soft brushes are used for cleaning and gently removing debris from the bonsai, ensuring that the tree and its pot are always presented at their best.
- **Tweezers**: Handy for removing dead leaves, unwanted buds, or debris, tweezers are a simple yet essential tool in bonsai maintenance.

Each tool in a bonsaist's workshop is an extension of the artist's hand, offering precision, control, and care. Proper use and maintenance of these tools make bonsai cultivation more enjoyable and reflect the practitioner's respect and dedication to this ancient art form.

13.2 Maintenance And Care Of Tools

The longevity and effectiveness of bonsai tools are greatly enhanced by proper maintenance and care. This subchapter focuses on the practices essential for keeping your tools in optimal condition, ensuring they continue to serve you well in the meticulous art of bonsai cultivation.

Cleaning and sharpening

Regular Cleaning: After each use, tools should be cleaned to remove sap, soil, and debris. This not only prevents the spread of disease but also keeps the tools in good working condition. A simple wipe with a clean cloth can be effective for daily cleaning.

Disinfection: Periodically, or when working with diseased plants, disinfecting your tools is crucial to prevent cross-contamination. Using a solution of diluted bleach or alcohol can effectively sterilize the tools.

Sharpening: Sharp tools make cleaner cuts that are healthier for the plant and easier to achieve. Regular sharpening of cutting tools, such as scissors and branch cutters, ensures precision in pruning and styling. Using a whetstone or a specialized sharpening tool can keep your blades in top condition.

Storage and handling

Proper Storage: Store your tools in a dry, clean place to prevent rust and corrosion. A toolbox or a storage rack can keep your tools organized and protected.

Handling with Care: Bonsai tools are often finely crafted and can be delicate. Handling them with care and respect prolongs their life and enhances your bonsai practice.

Regular Inspection: Regularly inspect your tools for signs of wear, damage, or rust. Early detection of problems can prevent further damage and the need for costly replacements.

Replacement and professional servicing

Knowing When to Replace: Over time, some tools may become too worn or damaged to repair. Knowing when to replace a tool is as important as maintaining it.

Professional Servicing: For more complex maintenance tasks, such as major sharpening or repairing damaged tools, seeking professional servicing can be a worthwhile investment.

Proper care and maintenance of bonsai tools are reflections of the bonsaist's dedication to their art. Well-maintained tools not only make the practice of bonsai more enjoyable but also embody the respect and reverence for the living art of bonsai.

13.3 Supplementary Materials For Bonsai

Beyond the essential tools, supplementary materials play a significant role in the art of bonsai. These materials, ranging from various soils to wires and decorative elements, contribute to the bonsai's health and aesthetic presentation.

Soil mixes

The choice of soil is crucial for the health of a bonsai. Different species have different requirements in terms of drainage, water retention, and nutrient content.

Specialized Bonsai Soil: Commercially available bonsai soils are formulated to provide the right balance for most bonsai trees. They usually contain a mix of akadama, pumice, and organic matter.

Custom Soil Blends: Some bonsaists prefer to create their own soil mixes, tailoring them to the specific needs of their trees. This can involve experimenting with various proportions of inorganic and organic components.

Wires for shaping

Wiring is a fundamental technique in bonsai for shaping and training branches.

Aluminum and Copper Wires: These are the most commonly used. Aluminum wire is more malleable and easier to work with, making it suitable for beginners, while copper wire, being more rigid, holds shapes better but requires more skill to apply.

Fertilizers

Fertilizers are essential for supplementing the nutritional needs of bonsai, given the limited soil volume.

Balanced Fertilizers: These provide an equal ratio of the primary nutrients – nitrogen, phosphorus, and potassium.

Specialized Bonsai Fertilizers: There are fertilizers specifically formulated for bonsai, designed to support their growth without promoting excessive foliage or root development that can be counterproductive in a miniature tree.

Moss and decorative elements

Moss and other decorative elements are often used in bonsai to enhance the aesthetic appeal and to create a more natural-looking miniature landscape.

Moss: It adds to the visual appeal, can help retain soil moisture, and indicates a healthy level of humidity.

Decorative Rocks and Figurines: These can be used to complement the bonsai, adding to its story and the overall display. However, it's important to use them sparingly to avoid detracting from the tree itself.

Drainage and humidity trays

Proper drainage is crucial for bonsai health, and trays are often used to catch excess water.

Drainage Trays: These sit under the bonsai pot, protecting surfaces from water and allowing excess water to drain away freely.

Humidity Trays: Filled with water and pebbles, they increase the humidity around the bonsai, beneficial for certain species, especially in dry indoor environments.

Incorporating these supplementary materials into your bonsai practice enhances the health and growth of your bonsai and its presentation. Each element, from the soil mix to the decorative touches, contributes to the overall harmony and balance of the bonsai, reflecting the care and attention to detail that bonsai cultivation entails.

CHAPTER 14: FROM SEED TO SPLENDOR: CULTIVATING YOUR BONSAI

Welcome to Chapter 11, "From Seed to Splendor: Cultivating Your Bonsai." This chapter embarks on a journey that begins at the very inception of a bonsai's life – the seed. Cultivating a bonsai from seed is a journey of patience, care, and profound satisfaction. It offers a unique opportunity to witness and guide the entire lifecycle of these miniature trees, from the earliest stages of germination to the full splendor of a mature bonsai.

In this chapter, we will explore the intricate process of bonsai propagation from seed. This path is less traveled, as it requires more time and patience than starting with pre-grown plants or saplings. However, the rewards of growing a bonsai from seed are immeasurable. It allows for a deeper connection with the tree, as you nurture it from its very beginnings and shape its development at every stage of growth.

14.1 Propagation From Seed

The journey of cultivating a bonsai from seed is a profound and rewarding experience, offering a unique insight into the natural cycle of life and growth

Understanding seed selection

Choosing the right seeds is the first critical step in bonsai propagation. Not all seeds are equal, and the choice depends on various factors, including the species of bonsai you wish to grow, the climate of your area, and the specific characteristics you desire in your bonsai. Some species are easier to grow from seed and are more suitable for beginners, while others may present more of a challenge.

The stratification process

Many bonsai seeds require a process called stratification to break their dormancy. This process involves simulating the natural conditions that seeds would experience in the wild through the changing seasons. Stratification typically involves exposing the seeds to a period of cold, which can be done by placing them in a refrigerator. This cold treatment prepares the seeds for germination by breaking down germination inhibitors.

Sowing techniques

Once stratified, the seeds are ready to be sown. This stage requires careful planning. The choice of soil is crucial; it should be well-draining yet capable of retaining enough moisture to encourage germination. The seeds are typically sown in shallow trays or pots. It's important to sow them at the correct depth, which varies depending on the size of the seed. Generally, larger seeds can be sown deeper than smaller ones.

Initial Care and Germination

After sowing, the seeds require consistent care. This includes maintaining the right level of moisture and ensuring they are kept at an appropriate temperature. The soil should be kept moist but not waterlogged, as excessive moisture can lead to rot. Germination times vary widely depending on the species and the conditions. Some seeds may germinate within a few weeks, while others can take several months or even longer.

Patience and Observation

Patience is key during this stage. Watching for the first signs of germination is a test of patience and attentiveness. Once the seeds begin to sprout, they enter the next critical phase of growth. The young seedlings will require careful monitoring, as they are delicate and vulnerable at this stage.

In summary, propagation from seed is a journey that requires knowledge, patience, and a nurturing touch. It's a process that connects the bonsai artist to the essence of nature, starting a journey spanning decades. This initial phase of bonsai cultivation is not just about growing a tree; it's about embarking on a journey of growth, learning, and discovery.

14.2 Initial Growth And Cultivation

Following the delicate phase of germination, as discussed in the previous subchapter, we now enter a critical stage in the bonsai's journey: the initial growth and cultivation. This phase is about nurturing the young seedlings, guiding their early development while allowing their natural characteristics to unfold.

Transition from Seedling to Sapling

As the seedlings emerge, they transition from a state of vulnerability to one of gradual strengthening. During this period, the focus shifts to providing an environment that supports healthy growth. This involves ensuring adequate light, which is crucial for photosynthesis and the plant's overall health. Seedlings typically require plenty of indirect sunlight; too much direct sunlight can be harmful at this stage.

Soil and Watering Considerations

The choice of soil, initially made for germination, continues to play a vital role. The young bonsai requires a soil mix that offers a balance of drainage and nutrient retention. Overwatering is a common pitfall at this stage; it's essential to maintain a consistent moisture level in the soil, allowing it to dry out slightly between watering. This practice encourages the roots to grow stronger as they search for moisture, fostering a robust root system.

First Steps in Training and Pruning

As the seedlings grow, initial training and pruning begin. This is a gentle process, subtly guiding the shape and structure of the bonsai while respecting its natural growth pattern. Initial pruning is usually minimal, focusing on removing any unhealthy or disproportionately large growth that may unbalance the young tree. The aim is to encourage a strong, well-proportioned structure that will serve as the foundation for future styling.

Adapting to the Plant's Needs

Each bonsai species has its unique growth rate and characteristics, and these should guide the cultivation approach. Some species may exhibit rapid growth and require more frequent pruning and repotting, while others grow more slowly and need less intervention. Observing and responding to the specific needs of your bonsai is crucial during this stage.

Building a Strong Foundation

This phase of initial growth and cultivation is about setting the stage for the future. It's a time to build a strong foundation that will support the bonsai throughout its life. This involves not only physical care but also developing an understanding of the plant's individual needs and characteristics. As the bonsai grows, it gradually reveals its potential and character, guiding the bonsai artist in shaping its future form.

In summary, the initial growth and cultivation phase is a period of nurturing and discovery. It's a continuation of the journey begun with seed propagation, marked by careful attention and responsiveness to the growing bonsai. This stage lays the groundwork for the tree's future development, shaping not just a bonsai but a living embodiment of nature's resilience and beauty.

CHAPTER 15: EXPERT ADVICE: AVOIDING COMMON MISTAKES

Welcome to Chapter 12, "Expert Advice: Avoiding Common Mistakes." This chapter is designed to help novice and experienced bonsai enthusiasts navigate the complexities of bonsai cultivation while avoiding common pitfalls. Bonsai presents unique challenges with its intricate balance of art and horticulture. Learning from common mistakes is a crucial part of the journey, offering valuable lessons that enhance both the bonsai's health and the cultivator's skills.

In this chapter, we will explore frequent beginner errors, providing insights into how to recognize and avoid them. This is not just about correcting mistakes; it's about understanding the underlying principles of bonsai care that prevent these errors from occurring in the first place.

15.1 Frequent Beginner Errors

Embarking on the bonsai cultivation journey is exciting and challenging, especially for beginners who are navigating this intricate art form for the first time. I

Overwatering and underwatering

One of the most frequent mistakes made by beginners is incorrect watering. Overwatering is particularly common, as enthusiastic new bonsai owners often worry about their tree drying out. However, too much water can lead to root rot and fungal diseases, which are detrimental to the tree's health. Conversely, less common underwatering can lead to dehydration and weaken the tree. The key to proper watering is understanding the specific needs of your bonsai species, as well as observing the soil's moisture level, rather than adhering to a rigid watering schedule.

Neglecting light requirements

Another error is not providing the appropriate amount of light. Each bonsai species has its unique light requirements, and failing to meet these can lead to poor growth, leaf drop, or a lack of vitality. Beginners might place their bonsai in inappropriate locations, either too dark or overly bright. Understanding the natural habitat of your bonsai species can guide you in providing the right amount of light, whether it's full sun, partial shade, or indirect light.

Improper pruning

Pruning is fundamental to bonsai shaping and maintenance, but it can be daunting for beginners. Common errors include over-pruning, which can stress the tree, or improper pruning techniques that lead to unsightly scars or hinder the tree's natural growth. Learning the basics of bonsai pruning, such as when to prune, how much to prune, and the proper tools to use, is essential for maintaining the health and aesthetic of the bonsai.

Choosing the wrong soil mix

The choice of soil is crucial in bonsai cultivation. Beginners often use regular garden soil or an inappropriate mix, which can lead to poor drainage and a lack of necessary nutrients. Bonsai soil needs to be well-draining yet capable of retaining enough moisture to sustain the tree. Understanding the specific soil requirements for your bonsai species and using a suitable bonsai soil mix can significantly impact your tree's health.

Misunderstanding fertilization

Fertilization is essential for the health of a bonsai, but it can be a source of confusion for beginners. Over-fertilizing can burn the roots and damage the tree, while under-fertilizing can lead to stunted growth and a lack of vitality. Beginners should seek to understand the specific nutritional needs of their bonsai and use a balanced approach to fertilization, considering factors such as the species, the season, and the tree's stage of development.

Ignoring pest and disease signs

Early detection and treatment of pests and diseases are crucial in bonsai care. Beginners might not recognize the signs of infestation or illness until it's too late. Regular inspection of the bonsai for any unusual signs, such as discolored leaves, sticky residues, or unusual growths, and learning about common pests and diseases can help in early detection and effective treatment.

In summary, while beginners are bound to face challenges in their initial bonsai cultivation journey, understanding and avoiding these common errors can lead to a more successful and fulfilling experience. Each mistake is an opportunity to learn and grow, and with patience and persistence, beginners can develop the skills and knowledge needed to cultivate beautiful and healthy bonsai.

15.3 Advanced Tips And Techniques

In the realm of bonsai cultivation, advancing beyond the basics opens up a world of nuanced techniques and deeper understanding. These advanced practices nofine the aesthetic qualities of bonsai buand

Mastering advanced pruning techniques

Advanced pruning is an art that requires a deep understanding of each tree's unique biology and growth patterns.

Defoliation: This technique is particularly useful for deciduous trees. Removing leaves stimulates the tree to produce a second set of leaves that are often smaller and more numerous. This improves the aesthetic of fine branching and allows light to penetrate deeper into the tree, promoting inner growth. Defoliation should be done carefully, as it can stress the tree, and not all species respond well to this technique.

Deadwood Techniques: Creating jin and shari adds a dramatic, aged look to bonsai. Jin is the process of stripping the bark from branches, creating the appearance of deadwood, while shari involves creating areas of deadwood along the trunk. These techniques replicate the natural wear that trees undergo in harsh environments. The key is to do this gradually, over several seasons, to avoid stressing the tree too much.

Refining wiring skills

Advanced wiring is about precision and foresight, anticipating how the tree will grow and responding accordingly.

Detailed Branch Positioning: This involves not just bending branches into position but considering how they contribute to the overall design. It's about creating depth, balance, and movement. Each bend and twist should have a purpose and contribute to the tree's story.

Layering Wires: For more complex shapes or to control thicker branches, layering wires can be effective. This involves applying wires of different thicknesses in layers, providing the strength needed to hold the branch while minimizing damage to the bark.

Root pruning and repotting

As bonsai mature, their root systems need careful management to ensure the tree remains healthy and the design is maintained.

Selective Root Pruning: This is about more than just keeping the tree small enough to fit in its pot. It's about maintaining a healthy root system. Removing too many roots can stress the tree, while not removing enough can lead to pot-bound roots that can't absorb nutrients effectively.

Root Grafting: This advanced technique is used to add roots to a tree, either to improve its aesthetic (such as adding surface roots for a more aged look) or to improve its health (such as adding roots to a part of the tree that's struggling).

Soil composition and fertilization

Advanced bonsai care involves tailoring the soil and fertilization to the specific needs of each tree.

Custom Fertilizer Blends: Depending on the tree's stage of development, its health, and the desired outcome (such as promoting flowering or fruiting), you might need to adjust the balance of nutrients in your fertilizer.

Foliar Feeding: This technique involves spraying a diluted fertilizer solution directly onto the leaves. It can be an effective way to provide nutrients to a tree that's stressed or not absorbing nutrients effectively through its roots.

Climate and environmental adaptation

Creating the right microclimate can be crucial, especially in challenging environments.

Microclimate Creation: This might involve protecting the tree from excessive sun, wind, or cold. Techniques can include using shade cloths, windbreaks, or even creating a humidity tray for trees that need more moisture.

Seasonal Adjustments: Understanding how your tree responds to each season and adjusting your care accordingly is crucial. This might mean changing the position of the tree to protect it from cold winds in winter or intense sun in summer, adjusting watering schedules, or changing the type of fertilizer you use.

Artistic and creative development

At an advanced level, bonsai becomes a deeply personal art form.

Exploring Non-traditional Styles: This could involve experimenting with unconventional shapes, incorporating elements from different styles, or even creating entirely new forms that challenge traditional bonsai norms.

Display and Presentation: The way a bonsai is displayed can dramatically affect its impact. This includes choosing the right pot, stand, and even the background against which the tree is displayed. Each element should complement the tree and contribute to the overall presentation.

Continuous learning and experimentation

The journey of mastering bonsai is one of continuous learning and adaptation.

Engaging with the bonsai community through clubs, online forums, or exhibitions can provide new insights and inspiration.

Experimentation is key. Don't be afraid to try new techniques or styles. Even failures can be valuable learning experiences.

In advanced bonsai cultivation, every decision, from how you prune a branch to how you display your tree, contributes to a deeper understanding of this art form. It's a journey that never truly ends, as there is always more to learn, more to try, and more beauty to create.

Balancing aesthetics and health

Advanced bonsai care is a delicate balance between maintaining the tree's health and achieving aesthetic goals. This involves:

Observing Growth Patterns: Understanding how your bonsai grows and responds to different care techniques is crucial. This knowledge allows you to make informed decisions about pruning, wiring, and styling that enhance the tree's beauty without compromising its health.

Responsive Care: Being responsive to the tree's needs is key. This means adjusting your care techniques based on the tree's response to pruning, wiring, and environmental changes. For example, if a tree shows signs of stress, it may be necessary to modify your approach, perhaps by reducing the frequency of pruning or altering the fertilization regimen.

Advanced soil management

As you gain experience, you'll learn that soil is not just a medium for growth but a crucial component of bonsai health.

Customizing Soil Mixes: Advanced bonsai artists often create soil mixes tailored to the specific needs of each tree. This might involve experimenting with different components to improve drainage, aeration, or water retention.

Understanding pH and Nutrient Availability: The pH level of the soil can affect nutrient availability. Advanced practitioners test the soil's pH and adjust it as needed to ensure optimal nutrient uptake.

Styling and Refinement

In advanced bonsai cultivation, styling and refinement are ongoing processes.

Creating Depth and Perspective: This involves not just shaping the tree but considering its overall composition. How does the tree look from different angles? Does it have a sense of depth and perspective? Advanced styling techniques can create a more three-dimensional, dynamic appearance.

Refinement Pruning: This is about fine-tuning the tree's shape. It involves selectively pruning to improve the tree's overall silhouette, enhance the structure of branches, and refine the foliage pads.

Advanced display techniques

The presentation is a significant aspect of bonsai artistry.

Choosing the Right Pot: The pot is integral to the bonsai's overall appearance. Advanced bonsai artists spend considerable time choosing a pot that complements the tree's style, color, and proportions.

Display Settings: How and where you display your bonsai can dramatically affect its impact. This includes considering the background, lighting, and even the humidity of the display area.

Lifelong learning and adaptation

Perhaps the most important advanced technique is the commitment to continual learning and adaptation.

Learning from Nature: Advanced bonsai artists often find inspiration in natural landscapes, observing how trees grow in different environments and incorporating these observations into their bonsai practice.

Experimentation and Innovation: Don't be afraid to try new ideas or push the boundaries of traditional bonsai styles. Innovation is a key driver of the art form's evolution.

In conclusion, advanced bonsai cultivation is a deep and rewarding practice that combines artistic expression with a profound understanding of horticulture. It's a journey that requires patience, observation, and a willingness to learn and adapt. As you progress, you'll find that bonsai is not just a hobby but a lifelong path of discovery and artistic fulfillment.

CHAPTER 16: SOURCING BONSAI MATERIAL

Embarking on the bonsai journey is an adventure that begins with a single, crucial step: selecting your starting material. This choice isn't just about picking a plant; it's about choosing a path. Whether you're drawn to the idea of sculpting a young sapling or nurturing a seed into a miniature masterpiece, each option opens up a unique set of experiences and challenges. Let's explore the landscapes where these bonsai beginnings can be found, from the bustling aisles of local nurseries to the quiet corners of specialized bonsai havens.

Imagine walking through a nursery or garden center. It's here, among the rows of vibrant greenery, that many bonsai journeys begin. You might find yourself drawn to a pre-bonsai, a young plant already showing promise with its interesting form and potential. Or perhaps it's the nursery stock that catches your eye, ordinary plants waiting for someone with vision to transform them into extraordinary bonsai. When selecting from these, look for the health of the plant, the allure of its trunk, and the potential dance of its branches. Remember, a strong foundation—a good nebari—is like the roots of your own bonsai journey, essential for balance and beauty.

For those who seek not just a plant but a piece of wisdom, specialized bonsai nurseries are treasure troves. These places are more than just shops; they're sanctuaries where each bonsai, from seedlings to mature specimens, has been cared for with expertise. Here, amidst the curated collection of potential bonsai, you can also find guidance and advice, enriching your understanding and connection to the art.

Then there's the call of the wild—the Yamadori. These are trees that have been shaped by the elements, their character forged by the wind, rain, and sun of their natural environments. Collecting Yamadori is a practice steeped in respect, both for the tree and its home. It's a reminder that bonsai is more than cultivation; it's a collaboration with nature. If you choose this path, remember to tread lightly, ensuring your actions are sustainable and ethical.

For the patient soul, there's the journey of growing bonsai from seed. This is the long road, filled with waiting and watching as nature slowly unfolds in miniature. It's a practice of patience and vision, offering the reward of knowing your bonsai in every stage of its life. While it may take years before your seedling is ready for its first styling, the connection you'll forge with your tree is unmatched.

And for those who are drawn to the immediate beauty of bonsai, refined trees offer a living artwork to bring into your home. These are trees that have been shaped and nurtured over years, sometimes decades, by skilled hands. They represent not just an investment of money but an investment in learning and appreciation. Caring for a refined bonsai is an ongoing lesson in attentiveness and respect for the art form.

Choosing your bonsai material is the first step in a journey that can last a lifetime. Whether you're guided by the thrill of transformation, the call of the wild, the slow unfurling of life from a seed, or the immediate connection with a living artwork, each path offers its own joys and challenges. As you stand at the beginning, consider not just the tree before you but the journey you're about to embark on. In bonsai, as in life, the path you choose is as important as the destination.

16.1 In My First Year, What Should I Focus On Or Prioritize My Investment?

Choosing your entry point into bonsai cultivation is a critical decision that shapes your journey. Here's an in-depth look at each option, focusing on the investment required, the time you'll spend to see results, and expanded considerations for each approach.

Buying Mature Bonsai:

- **Investment:** High ($200-$1000+ depending on species and quality)
- **Time to Spend to See Results:** Immediate.
- **Consideration:** While mature bonsai provide instant gratification and a complete aesthetic experience from day one, they require a significant financial investment. The higher cost also comes with the responsibility of maintaining the tree's health and form, which can be daunting for beginners. This option is best suited for those committed to learning about bonsai care and maintenance from the outset and willing to invest money and time into understanding the nuances of bonsai health and aesthetics.

Pre-Bonsai with Potential:

- **Investment:** Moderate ($50-$200 depending on potential and species)
- **Time to Spend to See Results:** Short to Medium (1-3 years).
- **Consideration:** Pre-bonsai balances affordability and the opportunity for personal involvement in the bonsai's development. This option allows beginners to practice shaping and styling techniques without the long wait associated with younger plants. However, it still requires patience and a willingness to learn about bonsai care. It's an excellent choice for those seeking to actively engage in bonsai shaping while managing a relatively modest budget.

1-3-Year-Old Seedlings:

- **Investment:** Low ($10-$50 for quality seedlings)
- **Time to Spend to See Results:** Medium to Long (3-5 years).
- **Consideration:** Starting with seedlings is a test of patience and commitment, offering the full experience of bonsai cultivation from the ground up. It's the most affordable option but demands a long-term perspective. This approach is ideal for enthusiasts who are fascinated by the journey of growth and development and are eager to learn about every stage of the bonsai lifecycle. It's a way to truly connect with the art form, understanding the slow and rewarding process of nurturing a tree from its infancy.

Nursery Stock:

- **Investment:** Low to Moderate ($20-$100 based on size and species)
- **Time to Spend to See Results:** Medium (2-4 years).

- **Consideration:** Transforming nursery stock into bonsai offers a practical balance between hands-on involvement and time to see results. It's an accessible starting point that allows for creative expression and learning without the high cost of mature bonsai or the extended wait of growing from seed. This route requires a keen eye for potential in ordinary plants and a readiness to learn pruning and styling techniques. It's perfect for those who enjoy the challenge of uncovering hidden beauty and are looking for a relatively quick path to achieving a bonsai aesthetic.

Yamadori (Collecting Wild Trees):

- **Investment:** Variable (often the cost is in the equipment and travel, $0-$100 for permissions and tools)
- **Time to Spend to See Results:** Immediate to Medium (1-3 years for recovery and initial styling).
- **Consideration:** Yamadori offers a unique and rewarding experience, profoundly connecting bonsai artists with nature. However, it requires understanding local ecosystems, permissions, and the ethical considerations of collecting wild trees. The process of acclimatizing and rehabilitating a collected tree can be complex and requires patience and care. This approach is suited for those with a deep respect for nature, a willingness to invest time in learning about tree health and recovery, and an interest in the stories that wild trees can tell through their shapes and forms.

Growing from Seed:

- **Investment:** Very Low ($5-$20 for seeds and initial setup)
- **Time to Spend to See Results:** Long (5+ years).
- **Consideration:** The journey of growing bonsai from seed is the epitome of patience and dedication to the art. It offers a deep, intrinsic understanding of the growth process and a unique sense of accomplishment. This method is for those who see bonsai cultivation as a hobby and lifelong passion. It requires a commitment to learning and adapting over the years and provides an unparalleled opportunity to shape a bonsai's development from the beginning. Ideal for the patient enthusiast who values the process as much as the final product.

CHAPTER 17: EXPLORE THE WORLD OF BONSAI ON YOUTUBE

If you're looking for additional resources and inspiration for your bonsai journey, YouTube is a great place to find a wide range of informative and engaging videos. Here are some of the top channels to follow:

1. **Bonsai Empire**
   Bonsai Empire's official channel offers a wealth of videos covering all aspects of bonsai, including detailed tutorials, beginner guides, bonsai garden tours, and much more.

2. **Herons Bonsai**
   With over 100,000 subscribers, Herons Bonsai is a valuable resource for bonsai enthusiasts. You'll find videos on topics such as pruning, styling, repotting, and more, presented by industry experts.

3. **Mirai Live**
   Mirai Live is the channel of Ryan Neil, a renowned bonsai expert. It provides access to online classes and seminars, allowing you to learn directly from one of the top bonsai masters in the world.

4. **Bonsai Iligan**
   This channel is run by Jerome Llaguno, a passionate bonsai enthusiast with extensive experience in the field. You'll find videos on bonsai cultivation, practical tips, and showcases of exceptional trees.

5. **Bonsai Network Japan**
   If you're interested in Japanese bonsai culture, this channel is a valuable resource. Explore Japan's most famous bonsai gardens, watch demonstrations by world-renowned artists, and immerse yourself in bonsai tradition and history.

These are just a few of the many YouTube channels dedicated to the bonsai world. Explore the content of each channel to find the ones that best suit your interests and learning needs. Happy watching and happy bonsai!

CONCLUSION

As we draw the curtains on "Bonsai for Beginners," we find ourselves not at the end, but at the threshold of a continuing journey. This book has been a comprehensive guide, a journey through the art and soul of bonsai cultivation, designed to enlighten, inspire, and guide enthusiasts at all levels of experience.

Bonsai is an art form that transcends typical gardening, inviting practitioners into a world of growth, patience, and discovery. Throughout the chapters, we've journeyed together through the essentials of bonsai care, delving into the selection of trees, understanding their unique needs, and exploring the delicate processes of pruning, wiring, and styling. Beyond just imparting practical guidelines, this book has aimed to instill a deeper appreciation for the ancient art of bonsai, highlighting its nuances and the profound satisfaction it offers.

The essence of bonsai cultivation lies in the art of patience and observation. As you nurture and shape your bonsai, it becomes evident that these miniature trees are not just plants but teachers, offering lessons in the rhythms of nature and the virtues of patience and attentiveness. Each day, they evolve and respond to your care, a new chapter in a shared story of growth and fulfillment.

Your journey in bonsai does not end here. Bonsai cultivation is a path of lifelong learning, a dynamic and ever-evolving art with new techniques to master and endless insights to gain from each tree. The bonsai community awaits with open arms, offering forums, workshops, and exhibitions where experiences and advice are shared freely. In every challenge faced, whether styling a stubborn branch or nursing a sick tree, there lies an opportunity for growth and learning.

Bonsai is also a canvas for artistic expression, a medium through which your vision, creativity, and emotions can be channeled. The styles and techniques you've learned are tools to help you express yourself through these living sculptures. Each tree reflects your journey, evolving with you, capturing the essence of your artistic expression.

As you close this book, see it not as a conclusion but as a companion on your ongoing bonsai journey. Its pages are there for you to return to, offering guidance, inspiration, and reassurance as you grow in this art. The journey with bonsai is a lifelong adventure that promises the beauty of miniature trees, a deeper connection with nature, and a profound sense of personal fulfillment.

In the bonsai world, every ending is a new beginning, every challenge a new opportunity. May your journey in bonsai cultivation be filled with growth, discovery, and joy. Happy cultivating!

Made in the USA
Las Vegas, NV
20 February 2025